The Zoni English System

Writing Team: Maria Aurora Villamater
Janice Baquiran Torres

Methodology Team: Janice Baquiran Torres
Maria Aurora Villamater
Hakan Mansuroglu
Zoilo C. Nieto

Editor: Hakan Mansuroglu

Director: Zoilo C. Nieto
Hakan Mansuroglu

Zoni English System 7: REAL SITUATIONS, Third Edition

Copyright © 2021, 2017, 2015, 2008 by Zoni Language Centers

All rights reserved. No part of this publication may be reproduced or transmitted in any form or by any means, electronic or mechanical, including photocopy, recording, or any information storage and retrieval system, without permission in writing from the publisher.

Requests for permission to make copies of any part of the work should be mailed to: Permissions Department, Zoni Language Centers, 22 W. 34th Street, New York, NY 10001.

Sales Department: U.S. and international: (212) 736-5544

Foreword

The Zoni English System has been designed as a classroom instructional method in response to the great need demonstrated by nonnative speakers of English in their everyday lives in English-speaking countries.

Since communication is essential for survival, the Zoni English System method is based on daily life situations, while explaining fundamental expressions as well as grammatical structures. In so doing, we have also employed high-frequency vocabulary. Effective textual materials increase the student's motivation to continue studying English by influencing his or her attitude toward learning as well as enhancing his or her future possibilities.

OBJECTIVES

The Zoni English System achieves the following objectives:

1. To reach out to students of diverse backgrounds
2. To create a universal program for anyone to learn practical English
3. To get students to produce immediate results in English
4. To get students to think in English
5. To encourage students to gain confidence in and lose any fear of the language
6. To keep student motivation high during the learning process
7. To build up students' fluency through participation and constant practice

Zoni English System, Real Situations features graphic-rich, student-centered-learning lessons that build on the previous Zoni English System topics and introduce new, high-usage material such as *future tense with time clauses, future perfect tense, if conditionals in the past, adverb clauses, rejoinders, phrasal verbs and idioms* and much more. A variety of creative and proven methodologies and techniques are utilized to facilitate the achievement of the Zoni English System objectives.

TO THE TEACHER

<u>In the classroom</u>
Teacher talking time 20-30%
Student talking time 70-80%

Techniques To Be Employed:

Instructors utilize such teaching techniques as:

- C.I.P.: Choral Intonation Practice
- Backward build-up (expansion) drill
- Elicitation
- Vanishing
- Interaction
- Role playing
- Commands to direct behavior
- Action sequence
- Student self-correction
- Student peer-correction
- Conversation practice
- Single-slot substitution drills
- Multiple-slot substitution drills
- Chain drills
- Transformation drills
- Teacher silence
- Word charts
- Structured feedback
- Positive suggestions
- Question and answer exercises
- Jigsaw (Cooperative Learning)
- Language games: feedback, party time, scavenger hunt
  (See the **Zoni Teacher's Manual**)
- Fill-in-the-blank exercises
- Match-the-meaning vocabulary exercises
- Reading and listening activities (See the **Zoni Teacher's Manual**)

Lesson plan/technique explanations are available for instructors.

Teachers who have not gone through the Zoni co-teaching program are required to follow the methodology and techniques detailed in the **Zoni Teacher's Manual**.

Important Symbols:

Teachers consult the **Zoni Teacher's Manual** for instructions

Teachers continue eliciting to complete the interaction with entire class participation.

Teachers make groups of two students for Pair Practice.

Zoni English System 7 continues the emphasis on regular group work in the classroom and facilitates the student-centered environment of the classroom. This is achieved through Group Work exercises where groups of three or more students work together on previously introduced material in a real communicative and cooperative learning environment. This increased importance placed on student-centered learning in the Zoni classroom supports the enhanced and simultaneous usage of all four language skills. Each student is given greater amounts of class time, thereby maximizing student learning and progress in the classroom. (See the **Zoni Teacher's Manual** for more discussion of the Group Work process)

CLASSROOM SEATING ARRANGEMENTS

In addition to applying various teaching methodologies, teachers are also encouraged to vary their classroom seating arrangements based on the lesson. The number of students and class size are factors that will also help to determine the seating arrangements.

Standard

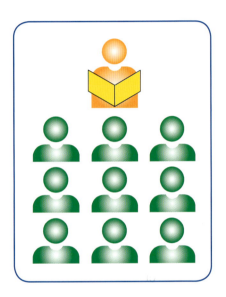

This type of seating arrangement, where students are arranged in rows, is generally used for lecture-type lessons and presentations. It is also beneficial when we need all the students to be focused on a particular task on the board. Students are able to work at their own pace while doing their assignments. It tends to be teacher-centered. The teacher must circulate and make lots of eye contact with his/her students to ensure all are involved in the assigned task.

In the Zoni System, lessons generally begin with the standard seating arrangement, especially during the introduction of a grammar point.

Semi-circle

This seating arrangement is recommended when maximum student interaction is required to focus on a particular task, such as getting information from the board or audio-visual activities and exercises. Students are able to see their classmates' gestures and facial expressions easily during discussions. In addition, it is less teacher-centered, so it provides lots of student interaction.

ZONI LANGUAGE CENTERS ©

Circle: Group Work

Group work generally consists of three or more students. There is maximum student participation. Students are more relaxed about experimenting with the language and the fear of making mistakes is diminished. Group work is a cooperative learning experience where students learn from one another. Group work becomes very effective when the groups are given clear instructions, tasks related to the objective of the lesson and a specific allotment of time in which to complete the assigned tasks.

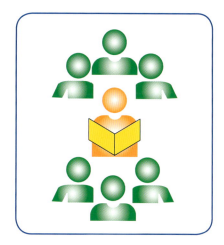

Pair Work

The same conditions exist as with group work but with 2 students.

In the lower and intermediate levels, the Zoni System incorporates a lot of group work and/or pair work during the practice period sessions.

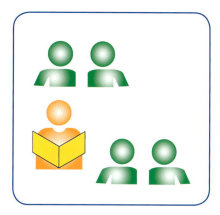

Homework

When we assign homework to students, it is important that we also check it in the following class. Checking homework should not take more than 15 minutes. Make sure you check all students' homework. Vary your checking homework routine; for example, check it in the second hour of class. Finally, keep a record of which students have not done their homework. For each assignment not completed, a student gets a zero. Alert any student who receives a lot of homework zeroes, as s/he may have to repeat the course.

Surprise Factor
Though developing a routine in the classroom is good, at other times, it is critical that teachers change their classroom routines to keep students on their toes.
Some ways to use the surprise factor are:

1. Checking the homework in the second hour of the class period instead of at the beginning of the class period.

2. Asking the class a question, then zeroing in and calling on a student to answer it.

Indispensable Oral Practice
The Zoni English System encourages choral and individual repetition in order to improve the students' pronunciation and to help them lose any fear of the language. Teachers should not be reluctant to practice pronunciation even with upper-level students; all students of any level benefit from this frequent practice. Teachers should also ensure that students keep their books closed and do not take notes during the introduction of a new subject or during oral practice. Their focus must remain on the task and subject matter.

Elicitation from the Students
Take advantage of students' prior knowledge by eliciting vocabulary and examples from them. By doing so, we share their knowledge with the rest of the class, build confidence, promote active thinking, and stimulate students to come up with interesting examples.

BOARD WORK

At Zoni, we believe in keeping board work as simple as possible, especially when teaching the beginner and intermediate levels. Board work is beneficial in that teachers can use it as a resource for student practice when doing Choral Intonation Practice (CIP), drilling and role-playing. Board work keeps students focused. Board work reinforces reading and spelling.

While doing board work, make sure all students have their books and notebooks closed. No writing or copying is allowed during this period. All students must be focused on the board. Write in print, not cursive. Plan what you will be putting on the board ahead of time. If writing a long dialogue, work your dialogue one segment at a time. We strongly recommend that teachers follow our board work examples displayed in the **Zoni Teacher's Manual**.

ATTENDANCE

Learning English is a matter of constant and consistent practice and dedication. Student attendance is vital for maximum learning and benefit; this is why teachers must remind students that regular attendance is necessary. If students do not comply, they may be asked to take the course again. Attendance should not be taken for granted. Encouragement and reminders about class attendance are essential.

ACKNOWLEDGMENTS

We are very pleased and proud to announce the publication of a new chapter of the Zoni English System series: *Zoni English System 7*. The experience of constantly challenging the status quo has led to the creation of this book. Many people have been involved in this project; their passion, persistence, dedication, and collaboration made it possible to complete *Zoni English System 7*. We would like to offer special thanks to **Masami Soeda** for her fabulous graphic-design work. Also, we would like to thank **Patricia Russo, Mae Liu, Max Sanchez, Melinda Ferrari** and **John David Zurschmiede** for their valuable input. We very much appreciate the cooperation and suggestions of the Zoni faculty. Further, we would like to thank **Evina B. Torres, Victoria Ochoa** and **Miyuki Adachi** for their review of this edition. In addition, we would like to recognize the contributions of Zoni students who have provided us with much-needed feedback.

Zoilo C. Nieto & Hakan Mansuroglu
Directors

TABLE OF CONTENTS

LESSON 1   TECHNOLOGY — 1

Grammar:	Future Tense with Time Clauses	8
Communicating Effectively:	Rejoinders I	14
	Rejoinders II	18
Idioms:	Discover the Meaning	21
Grammar:	Future Progressive Tense	27

LESSON 2   IMMIGRATION — 41

Communicating Effectively:	Stating Ideas/Starting a Statement	45
Idioms:	Discover the Meaning	48
Grammar:	Future Perfect Tense	53

LESSON 3   EDUCATION — 71

Idioms:	Analyzing Advertisements	74
Grammar:	Adverb Clauses of Time	80
Communicating Effectively:	When You Don't Understand	88
Grammar:	Adverb Clauses of Cause & Effect	90

LESSON 4 CAREER 105

Grammar:	**Adverb Clauses of Contrast**	**115**
Communicating Effectively:	**Expressing, Accepting & Rejecting Ideas**	**119**
Grammar:	**Adverb Clauses of Condition**	**122**
	Untrue Conditional in the Past	**125**
Idioms:	**Job Hunting**	**128**

LESSON 5 HEALTH 143

Idioms:	**Discover the Meaning**	**149**
Grammar:	**Noun Clauses with Verbs and Adjectives**	**157**
Communicating Effectively:	**Conversation Killers & Keepers!**	**162**
Grammar:	**Noun Clauses with Embedded Questions I**	**167**
	Noun Clauses with Embedded Questions II	**168**
	Noun Clauses with Embedded Questions III	**168**

APPENDIX

Verb List	**183**
Phrasal Verbs & Idioms	**185**

Dear Zoni Student

We would like to welcome you to the next course, High Intermediate, Real Life Situations. In order to get the most out of your study of English, you should always do the following:

- Speak only English in class.
- Attend class every day.
- Do all assigned homework.
- **Relax and have fun!**

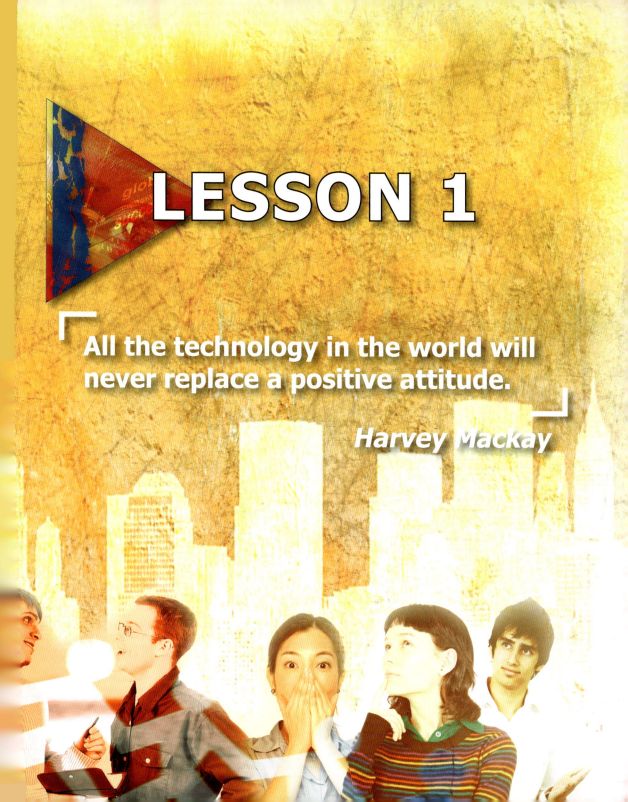

LESSON 1: Technology

GETTING THE PICTURE: Throughout recent generations, a lot of technological advancements have taken place: Cell phones have cameras, computer connections are wireless, and online education is now available. Discuss and deliberate on the following questions in groups of three or four. Answer the questions in complete sentences:

1. Take out any electronic gadgets that you have right now and explain to each other the benefits of owning them.

2. Do you enjoy the benefits of technology? Please explain.

3. People can't seem to live without iPods or video games nowadays. Do you believe that technology interferes with social interaction and reduces the time people spend with each other?

4. A language can now be learned through audio CDs, DVDs, phone apps or on the internet. How do you think people are going to learn a language in the future?

5. Given the power and resources, what would you invent for the benefit of future generations?

A. READING: Work with your group on the paragraph below and underline any new vocabulary. If needed, use an English dictionary to look up the meanings. Report your findings to the other groups.

Nowadays, we often hear people talk about the latest gadget or technology. Some eagerly wait in line to purchase the newest phone, iPod or television, while others wonder what the next exciting hi-tech device will be. With the rapid technological development that is taking place, there is no doubt that high technology will continue to increasingly take control over many aspects of our lives in the coming years. The modern technology we now enjoy has evolved from the inventions of the past. These inventions could not have come into existence if it hadn't been for their inventors. Alexander Graham Bell and Thomas Alva Edison are just two of the great inventors who have made our lives easier and more comfortable. On the next page, there is a graph that shows how technology has evolved over the years. In groups of three, analyze the graph and report the step-by-step evolution of each device to the class.

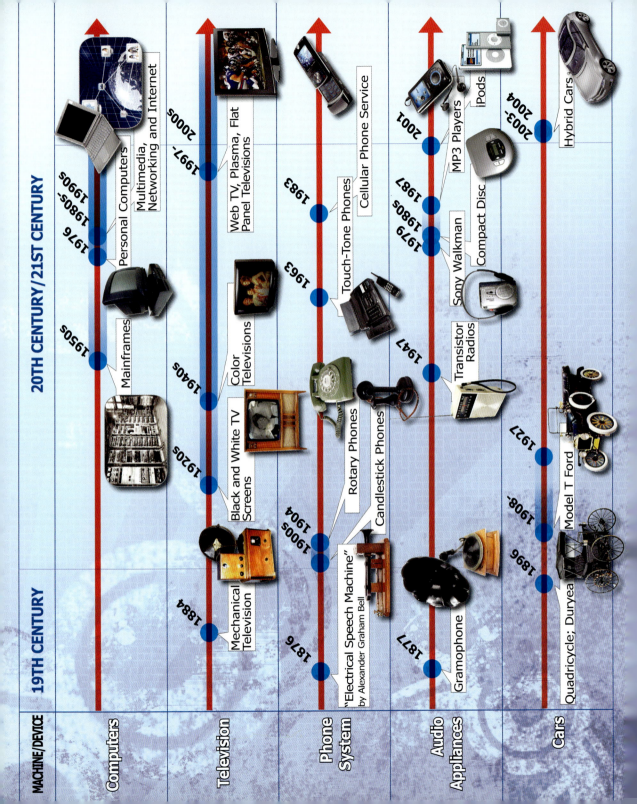

B. MEMORY GAME: Your teacher will divide you into Groups A & B. Each group must prepare five questions to test the other group.

Example: What year was the Walkman invented?

What kind of car existed in 1896?

C. Match the words with their definitions and/or synonyms by using contextual clues (figuring out the meaning of the word by the way it is used in a sentence.) Write the corresponding letter in the blanks provided. In addition, write the part of speech of each word - adjective, noun, verb or adverb - in the second blank.

COLUMN A	COLUMN B
1. gadget _f_ _noun_	a. one that precedes; forerunner
2. eagerly ____ ____	b. affording or enjoying contentment
3. rapid ____ ____	c. a thin television or computer screen made of tiny cells filled with gas and give off light when electricity passes through them
4. predecessor ____ ____	d. to change or adapt to the environment
5. comfortable ____ ____	e. very fast; very quick
6. evolve ____ ____	f. a small mechanical or electronic device
7. multimedia ____ ____	g. with enthusiastic or impatient desire or interest
8. networking ____ ____	h. using, involving or encompassing several types of media
9. mainframe ____ ____	i. the exchange of information or services among individuals, groups or institutions
10. plasma ____ ____	j. a large fast computer that can handle multiple tasks concurrently

ZONI LANGUAGE CENTERS ©

D. READING COMPREHENSION: Work in groups of three to discuss the questions below based on the previous reading activity. Report your answers to the class.

1. Who are two great inventors who have made our lives easier? Can you name other inventors? What are their inventions?

_____ : _____

_____ : _____

_____ : _____

_____ : _____

2. What type of car was invented in the 19th century?

_____

3. What devices were the predecessors of MP3 players and iPods?

_____

4. How has technology made our lives more comfortable?

_____

5. Do you think that technology will continue to have an increasingly large impact on people's lives in the future? Why or why not?

_____

E. HOMEWORK: Choose five words from the vocabulary list and use them in your own sentences. Report your sentences to the class.

Example:

multimedia - My father still keeps his old desktop computer. It's a dinosaur and it doesn't have any multimedia functions.

1. _____ - _____

2. _____ - _____

3. _____ - _____

4. _____ - _____

5. _____ - _____

FUTURE TENSE WITH TIME CLAUSES
Let's Break The Ice

LESSON 1

Work with your partner. Look at the two pictures and come up with a complete sentence using the given time expressions. Follow the example below.

Ex. SECOND ACTION

when

FIRST ACTION

Example: He will work for Microsoft **when** he graduates from college.

1. SECOND ACTION

before

FIRST ACTION

It's our first Plasma TV.
2. SECOND ACTION

after

We have to let it go.
FIRST ACTION

Jack — Thank you! — Naomi
3. SECOND ACTION

as soon as

Wow! — It's for you.
FIRST ACTION

PAGE 8   ZONI LANGUAGE CENTERS ©

 when

4. SECOND ACTION — FIRST ACTION

 as soon as

5. SECOND ACTION — FIRST ACTION

FUTURE TENSE USING TIME CLAUSES

A time clause uses **as soon as, when, before & after**. The verb in the **time clause** is in the <u>present tense</u> while the verb in the **main clause** is in the <u>future tense.</u>

Future Tense	as soon as when before after	Simple Present Tense

Examples:

Jennifer *will install* a security camera **before** she *moves* into her new house.
     (main clause)   (time clause)

Mr. Cho *is going to* sell his new invention **as soon as** the government *approves* it.
        (main clause)   (time clause)

Pair Practice

Connect the sentences using the time expressions in the parentheses below. Make sure the order of the sentences makes sense. Report your sentences to the class.

Example: I will buy a GPS device. I will receive my next pay check. **(when)**

I will buy a GPS device when I get my next paycheck.

1. Cell phones will have holographic displays. We will be old. **(when)**
   _____

2. My sister will pursue another degree. She will quit her current job. **(after)**
   _____

3. I am going to travel to Europe. I will get my bonus. **(as soon as)**
   _____

4. Rita will complete her college degree. She will find a high-paying job. **(after)**
   _____

5. I will leave for Canada. I will give you a goodbye kiss. **(before)**
   _____

6. He will settle down. He will find the woman of his dreams. **(when)**
   _____

7. Your parents will be glad. They will see your high score on your exam. **(when)**
   _____

8. My boss will give me a reward. I will finish my big project. **(as soon as)**

_____

9. Keith is going to invent a flying car. He will turn 80. **(before)**

_____

10. Carolyn will acquire a lot of properties. She will get married to a billionaire. **(when)**

_____

Party Time

Walk around and interview ten of your classmates to complete the sentences below. Make sure to use the appropriate time expressions in your answers.

Example: When will you get new shoes?

Hanako will get new shoes as soon as she _finds a sugar daddy_.

1. When will you purchase a house?

_____ will purchase a house when he/she _____.

2. When will you return to your country?

_____ will return to his/her own country

as soon as he/she _____ .

3. When will you be the happiest person on earth?

_____ will be the happiest person on earth

when _____ .

4. When are you going to look for a job?

_____ is going to look for a job when _____ .

5. When will you commit to a relationship?

_____ will commit to a relationship

after _____ .

6. When are you going to travel?

_____ is going to travel after _____ .

7. When will you throw a big party?

_____ will throw a big party

after _____ .

Homework

WRITING: Write about your future plans after you complete your English studies. Use the following time expressions in your composition: ***when, after, before*** and ***as soon as***. Read your composition in class.

My Future Plans

When I complete my English courses at Zoni, I will...

Communicating Effectively

REJOINDERS I

Below are examples of rejoinders used in different real life situations. Read each kind and add your own in each category. Share your answers in group or in class.

Rejoinders are short and quick responses given to the person you are having a conversation with to express interest and show that you are paying attention.

Basic rejoinders:

How are rejoinders used in the situations below?

1. When you hear good news:

> **EXAMPLE:**
> **Jenny:** "With the progress of technology, life will be easier when 2050 comes!"
> **Raschid:** That's great!

What other rejoiners can you use? Take note of your classmates' and teacher's responses:

_____   _____

_____   _____

Think of your own good news using future tense with time clauses. Then practice with your group. Each group member must react using a rejoinder. Role-play your dialogue in class using appropriate gestures.

2. When you hear bad news:

EXAMPLE: Sharon: "People are now too dependent on computers and other technology. The time will come when many people will be unemployed because almost everything is controlled by computers. In fact, my uncle got laid off when his company computerized its billing department."

Raschid: "Oh, I'm sorry to hear that."

What other rejoinders can you use? Take note of your classmates' and teacher's responses:

_____   _____

_____   _____

Make up some bad news using future tense with time clauses. Then practice with your group. Each group member must react using a rejoinder. Role-play your dialogue in class using appropriate gestures.

3. When you hear something shocking/surprising.

EXAMPLE: Mario: "Guess what, I will get a nose-job before I finish high school."
Danielle: "Are you serious?"

What other rejoinders can you use? Take note of your classmates' and teacher's responses:

_____   _____

_____   _____

Present your group with a shocking statement. Each group member must react using a rejoinder. Role-play your dialogue in class using appropriate gestures.

ZONI LANGUAGE CENTERS ©

4. **When you respond to ordinary statements:**

> **EXAMPLE:**
> **Libardo:** "I used to play soccer, but now I am more interested in baseball."
> **Raschid:** "I see."

What other rejoinders can you use? Take note of your classmates' and teacher's responses:

_____   _____

_____   _____

Share an interesting statement with your group. Each group member must react using a rejoinder. Role-play your dialogue in class using appropriate gestures.

_____

Let's see if the rejoinders you came up with are included in the list of most commonly used rejoinders below:

Good News	Bad news	Shocking	Ordinary
That's great! Awesome! Wonderful! _____ _____	I'm sorry to hear that. That's awful. That's too bad. _____	Are you serious? No way!!! Really?! You're kidding?! Are you kidding me? _____	Oh, I see. Oh yeah? That's interesting. _____ _____

Speed Dating

Write three sentences about your plans for the future using future time clauses. Then report them to another student who must respond using a rejoinder. Listen to your teacher's instructions.

My plans for tonight	Responses

My plans for tomorrow	Responses

My plans for the weekend	Responses

REJOINDERS II

Rejoinders can also be used in the form of short questions. Three examples are given below. You figure out the rest.

Examples:

My sister used to date Brad Pitt. → **She did?**
She didn't like him very much. → **She didn't?**

I want a new husband. → **You do?**

Hazan has married 5 times. → **She has?**

Your boyfriend calls me every night. → _____?

I'm really happy with my job. → _____?

My children are quadruplets. → _____?

Intonation note: Rising intonation is always used as shown above.

Stand Up

A. Write three sentences using different tenses. Then walk around the classroom and practice with different partners.

1. _____

2. _____

3. _____

B. Read the dialogue with a partner. Use the correct rejoinder question in each blank to complete the conversation below. When you finish reading, switch roles to practice again.

Student A: Hey Marty! I've been meaning to call you!

Student B: You have?

Student A: Yeah. I am really glad I ran into you because I have something to tell you.

Student B: 1.) _____? What is it?

Student A: Well, I know you collect DVDs. Yesterday, I was cleaning our storage and found some of my sister's old stuff. They're just collecting dust. You can have them.

Student B: 2.) _____? Won't your sister mind?

Student A: Not at all. In fact, she told me to throw them all away. But I remembered you. You see, she's such a pack rat. She keeps buying things she doesn't need.

Student B: 3.) _____?

Student A: Yeah. My mom has already spoken to her about it, but she's such a tough cookie.

Student B: Oh, 4.) _____?

Student A: She really is. That's why sometimes we don't **get along**.

Student B: 5.) _____?

Student A: We are very different from each other. I am very organized and she has no control over things. She's living a messy life. Her expenses are evidence enough. I bet she won't finish **paying off** her credit card balance for at least two years.

Student B: 6.) _____?

Student A: No way she can! She can't even **pay me back** what she owes me.

Student B: 7.) _____?

Student A: I **am fed up with** her and my parents can't seem to **put up with** her anymore.

Student B: 8.) _____?
Now I'm even more curious about her.

Student A: One day, I'll introduce you to her.

Student B: 9.) _____?
I have met her before.

Student A: 10.) _____?

Student B: Guess what, she's actually my girlfriend.

Discover the Meaning

Match the given idioms with their correct meanings. Refer to the dialogue for clues.

COLUMN A	COLUMN B
_f_ 1. be meaning to	a. to have a good relationship with
____ 2. run into	b. to be patient with
____ 3. collect dust	c. to be tired of something
____ 4. pack rat	d. someone who doesn't listen to others' advice; very stubborn person
____ 5. tough cookie	e. to completely pay a debt
____ 6. get along	f. to have been planning to do
____ 7. pay off	g. to remain unused for a long time
____ 8. pay someone back	h. to return what someone owes
____ 9. put up with	i. to meet by chance or accidentally
____ 10. be fed up with	j. someone who keeps everything, whether useful or not

Role Play

With a partner, complete each dialogue by filling in the right idiom. Then practice the dialogue together. Finally, role play the dialogue in front of the class.

1. Simon: "Hey Dave, I really need money to repair my desktop. I hope you don't mind me reminding you of the money I lent you."

David: "Don't worry, I will _____ tomorrow."

2. Ruby: "I'm having second thoughts about marrying Sam. He has to organize his life. He loves buying new electronics without getting rid of the useless items he has at home."

Janice: "Really? You mean he is a _____?"

3. Marcela: "Hey, Jerry. I have a problem. One of my students comes late every day. Not only that, he is on his phone during class. I already spoke to him, but he doesn't seem to take me seriously."

Jerry: "Uh-oh. You got a _____."

4. Paul: "Hello, Melissa! Have you read the novel I gave you?"

Melissa: "Oh that… I'm guilty. I haven't had time to do any reading these days. I've really been busy at work. So sad to say, the book you gave me is _____."

5. Robert: "Guess what! I saw Lisa at the mall last Sunday."

Takashi: "What a coincidence! I also _____ her the other day!"

6. Hazan: "There's just something about Jackie. I don't think we can be friends."

Steven: "Oh, I don't _____ with her either."

7. Irena: "Hi, Jun! I spoke to Julie and she was asking how you were doing."

Jun: "You spoke to her? That's great! Please tell her that I've _____ to call her, too!"

8. Christian: "I've been seriously thinking of buying a brand new Porsche."

Yukiko: "Hmmm… I suggest that you _____ all your credit cards first. What do you think?"

9. Beth: "So why did you move into an apartment?"

Sultan: "The repairs on the house never seemed to come to an end. I was _____ with it. I had already spent too much time and money."

10. Boyfriend: "I don't think we can work this out. You drink too much and I can't take it anymore. Let's cool off!"

Girlfriend: "Cool off? Let's break up! You think you're the only one having a problem with this relationship? I can't _____ with your extreme smoking habits anymore. I'll see you when I see you."

Let's Talk

Discuss the following questions. Use the opportunity to respond using rejoinders and idioms learned in this unit. Each student in the group must answer. Strictly speaking only. No writing!

TOOL BOX

Rejoinders

Are you kidding me?
Wonderful!
Oh, I see.
I'm sorry to hear that.
That's interesting.
Are you serious?
Awesome!
That's awful.
Oh yeah?
You're kidding?!
Really?!
That's too bad.
That's great!
No way!!!

Idioms

be meaning to
ran into
collect dust
pack rat
tough cookie
get along
pay off
pay someone back
put up with
be fed up with

SUGGESTED CONVERSATION PATTERN:

Example:

QUESTION: **A:** When will you get divorced? **(when)**

FUTURE TIME CLAUSE: **B:** I will get divorced when Brad Pitt proposes to me.

REJOINDER: **C:** Are you kidding me?

IDIOM: **B:** Why not? I think we'd get along.

1. When are you going to retire? **(when)**

2. When will you get a new car? **(before)**

3. When are you going to start working again? **(when)**

4. When will you go on vacation? **(as soon as)**

5. When are you going to treat me to lunch? **(when)**

6. When will your mother come for a visit? **(after)**

7. When is _____ going to buy a house? **(before)**

8. When will you call me? **(as soon as)**

9. When are you going to do the laundry? **(after)**

10. When will I see you again? **(when)**

Round Robin Story

Chain reaction using different time expressions. **(Ball toss)**

Example:

Teacher: I will watch a movie *when* I finish cleaning my room.

Student A: I will clean my room *before* I watch a movie.

Student B: I will go to bed *after*...

Student C: ...

FUTURE TENSE WITH TIME CLAUSES
Let's Break The Ice

JIGSAW: In five minutes, make as many predictions as you can on the topic your teacher will assign to you.

TV	**Ex:** People will be using hologram TV.
PHONE	**Ex:** We will no longer be using handheld phones.
COMPUTER	
CAR	
PERSONAL MUSIC PLAYER	

FUTURE PROGRESSIVE TENSE

The Future Progressive is used to express a continuous action (usually at a definite time) in the future.

$$\text{will + be + verb(-ing)}$$

YES/NO QUESTION:
Will you **be work**ing out at the gym at 8:00 tonight?

AFFIRMATIVE ANSWER:
Complete: Yes, I **will be work**ing out at the gym at 8:00 tonight.
   Short: Yes, I **will**.

NEGATIVE ANSWER:
Complete: No, I **won't be work**ing out at the gym at 8:00 tonight.
   Short: No, I **won't**.

INFORMATION QUESTION:
What will Apple, Inc **be introduc**ing next?
Apple, Inc **will be introduc**ing a new type of computer.

Guess Who

See Teacher's Manual

In pairs, pretend to be someone else (examples: husband and wife, doctors, business people, etc). Plan your day tomorrow based on your chosen characters. Write 4-5 sentences using the future progressive tense. Keep your choice of character a secret. Role play your sentences in front of the class and let your classmates guess.

Example: HUSBAND & WIFE

1. We will be preparing breakfast early.

2. We will be driving our kids to school at around 7:00 a.m.

3. We will be working until 5:00 p.m.

4. We will be picking up our children in the afternoon.

Practice

A. Fill in the blanks using the future progressive form of the verbs in parentheses. Report your answers to the class.

1. My husband will be very busy today because he **(work)** _____ on a project.

2. I **(give you a buzz)** _____ around this time tomorrow.

3. Don't bug Shirley tonight. She **(get ready)** _____ for her sister's birthday.

4. Do you want to join us? We **(check out)** _____ the newest cell phone models at the mall. Let's upgrade.

5. When did your best friend decide to work overseas? I'm sure you **(think about)** _____ her a lot when she is away.

6. I don't think Rebecca can join us tonight because she

(research) _____ her school paper.

7. A: Hey, John! Let's see a movie this afternoon.

B: I'm sorry. I'm afraid I can't join you because I **(look for)**

_____ a new computer for my son. What **(you,**

see) _____ ?

8. My dad **(drive)** _____ to Miami Beach around this time tomorrow.

9. My wife and I **(learn)** _____ a new language next month.

10. Wish me luck! I **(take)** _____ my TOEFL iBT exam this Friday!

B. Work with a group to complete the following sentences using the future progressive tense. Report your sentences to the class.

Example: At 3:00 tomorrow, <u>we will be studying online again</u>.

1. At this same time tomorrow, we _____.

2. Around 5:00 today, <u>(classmate's name)</u> _____.

3. In the morning, _____.

4. In five years, Microsoft _____.

5. Thirty years from now, _____.

6. Next year, _____.

7. I _____ this evening.

8. Don't call me at 10 a.m. because I _____.

9. In the next ten years, people _____.

10. Soon, Zoni Language Centers _____.

Charades: What will you be doing at _____ tomorrow?

Think of a verb and act it out in front of the class. Speaking is not allowed. Your classmates will guess what you will be doing at _____ tomorrow.

Example: SURF THE NET (ACTION)

Class's response: You will be surfing the net at 6:00 p.m. tomorrow.

Practice

Work in groups of three. Be a support group to a classmate who presents a problem. Give your best advice using the idioms you have learned and the future progressive tense when appropriate.

TOOL BOX : Idioms

be meaning to	get along
run into	pay off
collect dust	pay someone back
pack rat	put up with
tough cookie	be fed up with

1. I realized that I am in love with my friend, but he/she will be marrying his/her fiancé/fiancée in the next 3 months. I know there will be a lot of consequences if I tell him/her my true feelings. What should I do? Use my head or follow my heart?

Sample advice: I think you should use your head. You **will be ruining** his future plans if you tell him about your true feelings.

Advice:

2. My daughter will be moving into her own apartment next month. I don't think that she is ready to live on her own. She still depends on me to wash her clothes, cook for her and wake her up in the morning to go to work. I love her very much and I don't want to offend her. What should I tell her?

ZONI LANGUAGE CENTERS ©

Advice:

3. My husband and I will be celebrating our 10th wedding anniversary next week. I don't have enough money for us to go on a cruise. What could be a good anniversary gift?

Advice:

4. My neighbor will be going on a trip next weekend. He has asked me to take care of his dog. I want to help out my neighbor, but my roommate hates dogs. My neighbor has been very kind to me and I don't want to turn down his request. What should I do?

Advice:

5. I will be retiring in a couple of months. I am having second thoughts about it because I think I'll get bored. I am the kind of person who is always on the go and hates being idle. What do you suggest I should be thinking about doing?

Advice:

Bonus Activity

Work with a partner. For each statement check the box "**T**" (True) or "**F**" (False). Present your answers, with your reasons, to the class.

1. I am a tough cookie.
   - [ ] T   [ ] F

2. When I borrow money, I always pay it back on time.
   - [ ] T   [ ] F

3. I have been meaning to visit my country.
   - [ ] T   [ ] F

4. I can't put up with people who talk behind my back.
   - [ ] T   [ ] F

5. When I get fed up with my work, I take a vacation.
   - [ ] T   [ ] F

6. My grandmother is a pack rat.
   - [ ] T   [ ] F

7. I once ran into my ex-girlfriend/boyfriend with his/her new partner.
   - [ ] T   [ ] F

8. I don't get along with my boss.
   - [ ] T   [ ] F

9. I have cassette tapes that are collecting dust.
   - [ ] T   [ ] F

10. I've paid off all my credit cards.
    - [ ] T   [ ] F

Writing: Future Inventions

A. Draw a gadget that you would like to invent.

B. In one paragraph above, describe your future invention and why you want to invent it. Explain how it will benefit society and future generations.

C. Present your invention and read your paragraph in front of the class. Be ready to answer your classmates' questions.

Be A Detective!

Find the mistakes in the sentences below and correct them. Compare your corrections with your partner and present them in class.

Example: She will open a savings account as soon as she ~~is going to get~~ *gets* her allowance.

1. When my sister will get married, she is going to move into her husband's house.

2. **Maria:** Do you know that Criselda sold her dog?

   Jose: She was?

3. My family are going to be staying at the hotel during vacation.

4. She will don't use her computer today.

5. I give you big gift if you will graduate with honors.

6. Please don't go away. Your parents will missing you a lot.

7. His brother will joins us for dinner.

8. After she loan books from the library, she'll work on her term paper.

9. Levy: I understood this unit very well.

   Jonathan: You do? That's too bad.

Let's Debate!

Form two groups and debate one of the topics below in class.

- Computer systems negatively affect employment
- Outsourcing advances technological development
- The internet is detrimental to normal social interaction

Let's Google it!

Research the latest technology or gadget on the internet and report interesting findings in class. Bring a picture of your discovery if possible.

Quiz Yourself!

A. Choose the best way to complete each sentence:

1. David is going to invent a new gadget when…

      a. the government approves it.
      b. the government will approve it.
      c. the government approved it.

2. As soon as Mary lands in Europe,…

      a. she meets her new employer.
      b. she will meet her new employer.
      c. she met her new employer.

3. We will practice our dance…

      a. before we will perform.
      b. before we perform.
      c. before we are going to perform.

4. As soon as I get my bonus,…

      a. treat you to lunch.
      b. I treated you to lunch.
      c. I will treat you to lunch.

5. When we finish unit 1,…

      a. we will easily understand unit 2.
      b. we easily understand unit 2.
      c. we easily going to understand unit 2.

B. Complete the conversation with appropriate rejoinders:

1. Odes: Hi, Pete! Did you know that my daughter got me a new cell phone for my birthday?

Pate: _____

2. Ruby: I need a drink. My boyfriend broke up with me last night.

John: _____

3. Danny: Do you know that I have 14 children?

Doris: _____

4. Lyn: I work in New York and I live in New Jersey.

Leny: _____

5. Raschid: We've completed Unit 1 in this book!

Ozcan: _____

C. Complete the dialogue with the correct rejoinder questions:

Kriz: Hey! Evina called me from China last night!

Eduardo: _____? How's she doing?

Kriz: Well, she said she's doing really well there. We talked for like an hour and a half.

Eduardo: So what's new with her? I really miss her.

Kriz: _____2_____? We talked about so many things. One of them was the new car she bought 3 months ago. She has paid it off in full.

Eduardo: _____3_____? What a lucky girl. She must be earning a lot. I am so jealous.

Kriz: _____4_____? I am, too. Hey, why don't we visit her? What do you think?

Eduardo: Hmmm… not a bad idea. But actually, I can't. I'm really broke.

Kriz: _____5_____? I can lend you the money.

Eduardo: _____6_____?

Kriz: Of course I can! It'll be worth it to see Evina. She'll surely be surprised! She'll let us stay with her when we visit.

Eduardo: _____7_____? That's really great! This is interesting! Last night, I was thinking about going there.

Kriz: _____8_____? Then there's really no reason to delay the visit. Let's go online and buy the tickets now!

Eduardo: Let's go then! Uhm… wait. I think Rebecca wants to go, too.

Kriz: _____9_____? I will call her tonight. She went to China 3 months ago, though.

Eduardo: _____10_____? Let's invite her anyway. I am really excited. So???

Kriz: All right! Sounds like a plan!

D. Complete the sentences using the future progressive tense.

Example: Max __will be working__ **(work)** on the computer when his mother comes home.

1. Peggy _____ **(attend)** the conference on Saturday.

2. We _____ **(meet)** with the company's CEO tomorrow.

3. This time next week they _____ **(withdraw)** from the game.

4. At 6 o'clock on Friday she _____ **(sing)** her favorite song at the karaoke bar.

5. It _____ **(probably/rain)** when I reach Boston.

6. Tomorrow at nine I _____ **(give)** a speech to all the seniors at my university.

7. My children _____ **(watch)** a video when I arrive home tonight.

8. I _____ **(propose)** a new plan to my boss so I can get promoted soon.

9. She _____ **(replace)** her old cell phone soon.

10. They _____ **(broadcast)** the news using high definition technology.

Check your answers with the class. Count your points and check your score.

POINTS	PERCENTAGE	POINTS
25-30	90% - 100%	Great job!
20-24	75% - 85%	Very good!
15-19	65% - 70%	Good!
14 and below	60% - below	Study harder

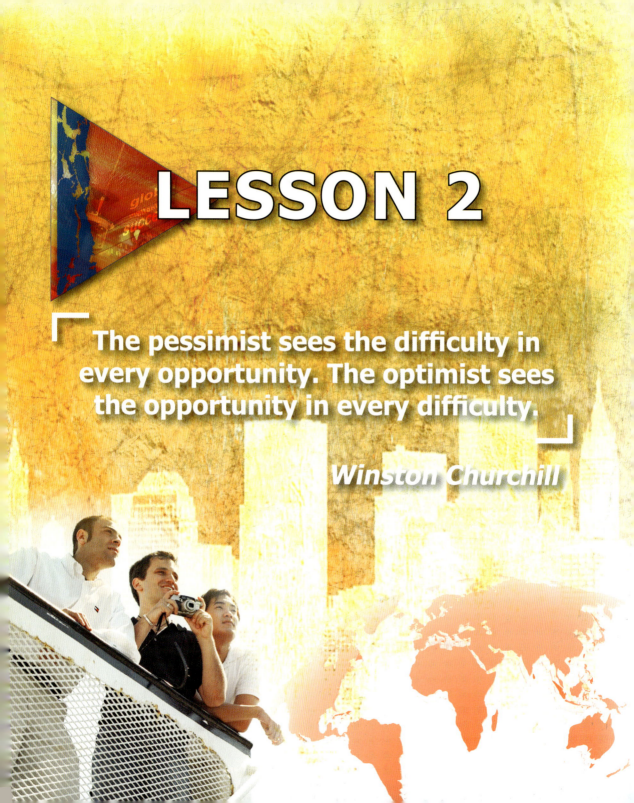

Immigration

Many people have left their countries in search of a better life in other countries. Many of them have made their dreams come true. Discuss the following questions in groups of three and answer in complete sentences. Share your opinions with the rest of the class.

1. Why do people **emigrate from** their countries and **immigrate to** other countries? List as many reasons as you can.

2. Which countries do most people from your country immigrate to? List all the countries that apply and discuss reasons why they choose those countries.

3. What difficulties do people encounter when moving from one country to another?

4. What are the pros and cons of living in another country?

5. Do people in your country look up to people who work or live in another country? Why or why not?

6. How does an immigrant become a citizen in your country? In the U.S. or Canada?

A. READING: In groups of four, assign each member of your group a role and read the conversation. Underline new vocabulary as you read. Share the new vocabulary words and figure out their meanings.

Hannah: **You know what**, many of my relatives have left for another country. My aunt just got a job in Japan and my cousin is now working in Taiwan. There's also a huge demand for nurses in the UK, so my sister is going, too. Is it really better to live in another country? I **don't get it**.

Charles: **By and large**, many people think that there are **greener pastures** somewhere else. Some of them prevail, and sad to say, some do not. Not all people who leave their countries find the kind of life they expect in another country.

Reynaldo: **As far as I can tell**, it's all about the economy and career opportunities. Many people are able to land high-paying jobs and earn a lot more overseas than in their own countries. In addition, their children receive better education in most cases. So I don't blame parents who leave their countries **for the sake** of their children.

Jerry: **In my mind**, a person can be successful without leaving his or her own country. Why should I leave my beautiful homeland that defines who I am?

ZONI LANGUAGE CENTERS ©

Hannah: **As a rule**, people leave to use their skills in another country and earn more. Well, I can only **shake my head**.

Charles: Hold on... hold on. **Basically**, there are many reasons why people immigrate. They can be economic, social, political, or environmental.

Reynaldo: **I'm afraid that** I don't **follow you**.

Charles: Okay. Economic is when someone moves to find a job and follow a career path. Like nurses, teachers, and computer programmers. They move to **make a living** where their degrees or skills are **in demand**.

Jerry: So what about social migration?

Hannah: Let me try. From the word "social," I guess social migration is when someone moves closer family or friends. Am I right, Charles?

Charles: Right. **You see**, moving to another country is not just all about money. It could be to be with a person you love or to meet new people.

Reynaldo: Political migration?

Charles: **Well**, political migration means escaping from war or political persecution. Like during the 17th and 18th centuries, Europeans migrated to the U.S. for political and religious freedom.

Jerry: Let me guess, environmental means to change the environment?

Charles: Something like that. But it's more than that. It basically means moving due to natural disasters like hurricanes, volcano eruptions, tornados, or earthquakes.

Hannah: Wow, what a great conversation. I've really learned a lot!

Reynaldo: So did I. Now I understand better why some people immigrate.

Charles: That's right. If you ever decide to immigrate to another country for whatever reason, there will always be **pros and cons**. Just do your homework beforehand.

B. COMMUNICATING EFFECTIVELY: Stating ideas/Starting a statement

From the conversation you just read, list the strategies in stating ideas or opinions. Then, come up with more expressions of stating ideas.

Example:

_____ You know what... _____ Let me tell you...

_____ _____
_____ _____
_____ _____
_____ _____
_____ _____
_____ _____
_____ _____

Pair Practice

Student A: Read the statements out loud to Student B.
Student B: Respond to Student A's statements using expressions from the tool box below.

TOOL BOX : Expressions

You know what	As a rule
By and large	Basically
As far as I can tell	I'm afraid that
In my mind	Well

1. **Student A:** Many people want to escape poverty in their own countries, so they move somewhere else to live a better life.

   Student B: <u>You know what, I still want to stay in my hometown no matter what.</u>

2. **Student A:** I know a lot of people who have left their countries to work in other countries, but have been unable to use their professional skills and are obligated to do different types of work.

   Student B: _____.

3. **Student A:** Do you think it's difficult to adjust to a new country's culture?

   Student B: _____.

4. **Student A:** I heard that homesickness is the number one enemy of a foreigner.

   Student B: _____.

5. **Student A:** Learning a culture helps when learning a language.

   Student B: _____.

Round Robin Story

A student makes a statement. Then another student responds with a conversation strategy in stating ideas or opinions. Later, another student makes another statement and so on, until everyone in class has participated.

Start

Student A

EX: You know what, I don't think I can live in another country. I still want to stay in my homeland.

Student B

In my mind, people should be able to live wherever their hearts desire.

Student C

As far as I'm concerned,...

Student D

As a matter of fact,

Student E

To be perfectly honest,

Student F

To tell you the truth,

Student G

In my opinion,

Continue...

ZONI LANGUAGE CENTERS ©

Discover The Meaning

Underline the group of words that can be changed into one of the idioms in the reading. Then write the correct idiom in the blank. The first item was done for you.

1. Immigration can be good and bad because there will always be <u>advantages and disadvantages</u> to living in another country.

   pros and cons

2. Juanita divorced her husband so she could get married in the U.S. again. They used to be such a happy couple. It makes no sense to me!

   _____

3. Did you know that nurses are greatly needed in the U.K.?

   _____

4. Why is it so hard to get a visa? I can't understand!

_____

5. You know what, Peter doesn't really want to be away from his family. He's just doing this for the benefit of his children.

_____

6. I don't think I can afford to buy a house yet. I am still not earning enough. Maybe later when my boss notices my great potential and gives me a promotion.

_____

7. Sometimes, Justyna's opinions are out of this world. That's why I don't understand what she is talking about most of the time.

_____

8. How can you earn money watching TV all day?

_____

9. Oh boy! I'm so nervous. It's my first visit to New York and I don't know what to expect. I'll just think positive! If I can make it there, I can make it anywhere.

_____

10. Do you really think there's a better and more exciting job somewhere else?

_____

Pair Practice

Work with a partner and take turns responding to each of the questions by using the indicated idiom. Use the appropriate tenses.

Example: (pros and cons)

A: Do you like living abroad?

B: <u>Well, it has its **pros and cons** but I think I've already adjusted well, so this country is my new home</u>.

1. (greener pastures)

    A: Why did Jonah quit his job? He was really good at it.

    B: _____

2. (in demand)

    A: A lot of nurses and teachers in my country have been recruited by an employment agency. I'm thinking of becoming a nurse too.

    B: Why? You were never interested in the medical field.

    A: _____

3. (make a living)

    A: Why do you have three jobs? Are you able to have a social life?

    B: _____

4. (for the sake of)

    A: It wasn't my idea to come here to the United States, but I just had to do it.

B: Why did you come here?

A: _____

5. (hope for the best)

A: My life is a mess! I just lost my job and I have a lot of bills to pay. What's more, my boyfriend and I just broke up. What am I going to do?

B: _____

6. (don't get it)

A: The government decided to give driver's licenses to undocumented immigrants. What do you make of that?

B: _____

Homework

Choose five idioms from the list and use them in your own sentences. Report your sentences to the class.

Example:

pros & cons - There will always be pros and cons to every decision we make.

1. _____ - _____
2. _____ - _____
3. _____ - _____
4. _____ - _____
5. _____ - _____

Lights, Camera, Action!

ROLE PLAY: In groups of three or four, create a dialogue on one of the topics given below. Use expressions in stating ideas and idioms in your dialogue. Role play the dialogue in class.

1. Working overseas
2. Getting a visa
3. Changing citizenship
4. Adjusting to a different culture
5. Learning English in the US
6. _____

Example: Topic – Learning English in the U.S.

Student A: Hey Anna! What's up? You know what, I want to learn English, but I can't seem to improve much.

Student B: Really? Let me guess. It could be because you hardly practice it with people.

Student C: As far as I can tell, it's easier to learn if you are in an environment that uses the language.

Student D: Well, actually, I improved a lot when I lived in Canada.

FUTURE PERFECT TENSE

Stand up and interview five people by asking:
"What will you have done by the time you turn 65?"
Write your interviewees' answers below. Report your findings to the class.

What will you have done by the time you turn 65?

__Anna__ : Anna will have retired by the time she turns 65.

_____ : _____

_____ : _____

_____ : _____

_____ : _____

_____ : _____

Future Perfect Tense

An action that will be completed before another time or event in the future.

> Will + Have + Past Participle of the Verb

Example:

I **will** *have saved* a lot of money by the time I return to my country.

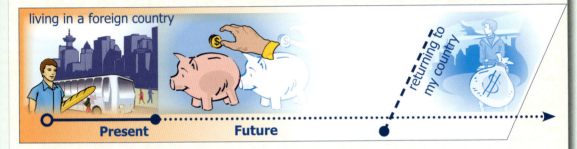

YES/NO QUESTION:
Will you **have perfected** your English by the time you complete your English studies?

AFFIRMATIVE ANSWER:
Complete: Yes, I **will have perfected** my English.
　　Short: Yes, I **will**.

NEGATIVE ANSWER:
Complete: No, I **won't have perfected** my English.
　　Short: No, I **won't**.

INFORMATION QUESTION:
How many countries **will** you **have visited** by the time you turn sixty?

Pair Practice

Using the future perfect tense, complete the sentence in each item with the given clues.

1. My best friend has lived in Australia since February.

By August, _____

2. Right now, it's 20___. Jimmy has worked in Taiwan for 10 years.

By 2030, he will _____

_____

3. Sandra started eating at 10:00 a.m.

By 11:30 a.m., she will _____

_____

4. That hospital was opened in 1930.

By the end of this year, it _____

5. It's been 3 hours since 3:00 p.m. and I have watched 2 movies already.

By 9:00 p.m., I will _____

_____

Jigsaw

In groups of four or five, complete the following sentences with your own predictions using the future present tense. Then listen to your teacher's instructions.

Example:
By the year 2030, <u>we will have returned to our country.</u>

1. By 2050, _____

2. By the time we finish all our courses at Zoni, _____
_____

3. By next year, _____

4. By the end of this year, _____

5. By the time we finish our class today, _____

6. By _____(time), _____

7. By tomorrow morning, _____

8. By the time I get home, _____

9. By tomorrow, _____

10. By the time our teacher comes in tomorrow, the students...
_____

LEND ME YOUR EARS

 Listen to your teacher carefully. Then choose the statement that is true according to the information you hear. Circle your answer.

1. a. Mario gets married in 2040.
   b. Mario gets married before 2040.

2. a. New immigration policies are imposed before the next 5 years.
   b. New immigration policies are imposed 5 years later.

3. a. Many nurses will get their green cards in March.
   b. Many nurses will get their green cards before March.

4. a. Maria will receive the flowers before noon.
   b. Maria will receive the flowers at noon.

5. a. I will go back to Manila before February.
   b. I will go back to Manila in February.

6. a. Maria's husband will get home before she finishes her homework.
   b. Maria will finish her homework before her husband gets home.

7. a. Hanna will get married before we leave for Japan.
   b. Hanna will get married after we leave for Japan.

8. a. My son will finish high school before this summer.
   b. My son will finish high school after this summer.

9. a. You will visit, then Sheila will leave.
   b. Sheila will leave, then you will visit.

10. a. She will finish her homework when mom gets home.
    b. She will finish her homework before mom gets home.

Party Time

Interview ten of your classmates to answer the following questions. Answer in complete sentences. Then report your findings to the class.

What will you have done by...

Example: ...the time you get home?

Maria: <u>I will have done my grocery shopping by the time I get home.</u>

Report: <u>Maria will have done her grocery shopping by the time she gets home.</u>

1. ...tomorrow?

   _____: _____

   Report: _____

2. ...the time you get home?

   _____: _____

   Report: _____

3. ...the age of 50?

   _____: _____

   Report: _____

4. ...the time you get married?

   _____: _____

   Report: _____

5. ...the time you get on the bus or train?

NAME: _____

Report: _____

6. ...2030?

NAME: _____

Report: _____

7. ...next year?

NAME: _____

Report: _____

8. ...the end of this year?

NAME: _____

Report: _____

9. ...8 o'clock tonight?

NAME: _____

Report: _____

10. ...the time your teacher enters the room tomorrow?

NAME: _____

Report: _____

Pair Practice

Complete the dialogues by using the simple future or future perfect tense with the verbs in parentheses. Compare your answers with a partner, then practice the dialogues together. Finally, role play the dialogues in front of the class.

1. Hasan: Do you think everything will be finished when I get back from the dry cleaners?

Tricia: Don't worry. By the time you get back, I (arrange)_____ the living room and (set)_____ the table. Everything will be ready.

Hasan: I hope so. They (arrive)_____ around 6 o'clock.

Tricia: Everything (be)_____ spotless by the time they get here.

2. Pei-ling: I have just two more courses to finish before I graduate from college. By this time next year, I (graduate)_____, and I will already be looking for a job.

Marcela: Isn't that scary? We'll be working in the real world. Are you worried about the future?

Pei-ling: Not really. I **(go)**_____ to a career counselor and get some advice on how to find a good job.

Marcela: That's a great idea.

Pei-ling: I am also going to do an internship so that when I leave school, I **(not only, complete)** _____ all my courses, but I **(also, gain)** _____ some experience.

3. Joe: Did you hear that Mike **(take)**_____ a vacation in Europe this summer?

Eden: I can't believe how often he goes abroad! Where exactly does he want to go?

Joe: He **(go)**_____ to Germany, Great Britain and Spain.

Eden: He really is a jet-setter. He **(visit)** _____ every country in the world by the time he's 50 years old.

ZONI LANGUAGE CENTERS ©   PAGE 61

4. Sima: How long have you been in Miami?

George: I have only been here for a couple of days.

Sima: How long do you plan on staying?

George: Well, I came here on a business trip but I think I **(stay)** _____ here for an extended period of time. Maybe about 3 more weeks. I deserve a break since I've been working like a dog.

Sima: Wow, that's quite a vacation! You **(definitely, see)** _____ just about everything there is to see in Miami by then.

5. Lisa: I can't believe how late we are! By the time we get to the dinner party, everyone **(finish, already)** _____ eating.

Ben: It's your fault. You spent hours fixing your hair and putting on makeup.

Lisa: Of course! I want to look my best in front of all the guests.

Ben: Who cares? By the time we get there, everyone **(leave)** _____. Nobody **(even, notice)** _____ your pretty hair.

HOMEWORK: FIND THE WORDS!

Find the past participles for each of the verbs listed below in the given box. Circle the past participles in the puzzle and write them next to their base forms.

1. pay   *paid*
2. catch
3. take
4. speak
5. broadcast
6. break
7. fall
8. sing
9. sting
10. feel
11. show
12. fly
13. make
14. hear
15. steal
16. shoot
17. get
18. beat
19. find
20. blow

P	C	D	S	H	O	W	N	W	B	F	A	C	F	B
A	Y	S	P	X	Z	E	J	E	R	A	M	A	L	R
I	H	F	O	U	N	D	B	L	O	W	N	U	O	O
D	N	V	K	P	C	U	A	E	K	Z	M	G	W	A
M	A	D	E	F	S	T	O	L	E	N	J	H	N	D
A	K	M	N	R	H	A	L	O	N	O	Y	T	S	C
S	K	R	F	J	O	K	W	C	G	Y	L	R	T	A
U	S	B	E	A	T	E	N	L	E	Q	L	V	U	S
N	F	A	L	L	E	N	S	G	O	T	T	E	N	T
G	E	I	T	O	H	E	A	R	D	G	R	Z	G	Z

ZONI LANGUAGE CENTERS ©

Conversation Practice

Discuss the following questions in groups of three. Use the opportunity to respond using conversation strategies and idioms learned in this unit. Each student in the group must answer. Strictly speaking only. No writing!

SUGGESTED CONVERSATION PATTERN:

Example:

QUESTION: A: What will you have accomplished by 20____?

FUTURE PERFECT TENSE + CONVERSATION STRATEGY: B: Well, by 20___, I will probably have completed my bachelor's degree.

IDIOM: C: Wow! With that, I'm sure you'll find greener pastures.

1. Where will you have traveled by the time you reach the age of _____?

2. What will you have done by the time you go to bed tonight?

3. How long will you have lived in the U.S. by the time you go back home?

4. How old are you now? How many years will your parents have been married by the time you turn _____ years old?

5.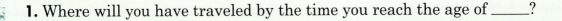

Writing

Draw a timeline of your plans or what you hope to accomplish in the next ten years.

20__ Study English at ZONI Language Centers

10 years later

In one or two paragraphs, write how you plan to accomplish your goals and why you want to accomplish them. Use the future perfect tense in your writing. Share your composition in class.

ZONI LANGUAGE CENTERS ©

Be a Detective

Underline and correct the errors in the sentences below. There could be more than one error in each sentence.

Ex: My father will ~~has return~~ from Iraq by the time I move out of the house.
    have returned

1. By the time I come back to my country, I will have complete my bachelor's degree in London.

2. My sister will has gave birth to her second child by the time her husband's contract in Saudi Arabia finishes.

3. I work late now. By the time the sun will set, I will have gotten out of the office.

4. I know you're hungry but don't worry. Kimberly will cook dinner by the time you get home.

5. I will have be married for one year by next June.

6. Oh, no! Heavy traffic! By the time we get to the airport, the plane will have leave!

7. Millions of nurses and doctors will have migrated to other countries by the time Lucy will finish her nursing degree.

8. By the time Eugene returns to his country, he is away from his family for more than 5 years.

9. You've promised you'll give me your computer since last year. I won't wait anymore. It will surely has get old by the time you give it to me.

10. We will understood this unit well by the time we finish this exercise.

Let's Debate!

Form two groups and debate one of the topics below in class.

- There is a relationship between immigration and crime
- The government should limit the number of immigrants entering the country
- Local culture is threatened by immigration
- Immigrants should have the same rights as citizens

Let's Google it!

Research the latest immigration issues in the United States, Canada or in other countries and report interesting findings in class.

Suggested topics:
- Jobs in demand in particular countries
- Deportation issues
- The different ways of becoming a permanent resident in different countries

Quiz Yourself!

A. Change the bold words into the appropriate idioms using the word bank on the next page.

1. **I don't understand**.

2. Aneta works hard **because of the needs of** her children.

3. Honey, I can't work alone. You have to help me **earn money to survive**!

4. My dad **is struggling with** my brother's decision to marry that woman.

5. There are **good and bad things** about working on weekends.

6. Jenny **can't understand** the professor because he speaks too fast.

7. Let's **think positively**!!!

8. I am one of the **ordinary workers** in this company. I'm not a manager.

9. Do you really think that there are **better opportunities** in another country?

10. I heard that teachers are **really needed** in New York.

Word Bank

I don't get it	hope for the best
greener pastures	rank and file
for the sake of	shake one's head (over)
follow someone	make a living
in demand	pros and cons

B. Fill in the blanks with the future tense or future perfect tense. Read the sentences carefully before writing your answer.

1. Maria _____ a huge farm in Houston, Texas next year. **(purchase)**

2. My son _____ by the time his father visits him from Europe. **(graduate)**

3. Aneta _____ in 2030. **(retire)**

4. My best friend _____ a lot of properties by the time she reaches the age of 40. **(inherit)**

5. By the time I reach the age of 80, my grandsons _____ **(accomplish)** a lot.

6. Robert _____ **(return)** to Nicaragua at 90.

7. My husband and I _____ **(volunteer)** to do medical relief work.

8. Bessy _____ **(complete)** her PhD by the time I give birth to my 3rd baby.

9. By next month, my brother will have already _____ **(sell)** 12 brand new cars in his new job.

10. Next month, Dixie _____ **(trade in)** her BMW for a brand new Acura.

Check your answers with the class. Count your points and check your score.

POINTS	PERCENTAGE	POINTS
18-20	90% - 100%	Great job!
15-17	75% - 85%	Very good!
13 - 14	65% - 70%	Good!
12 and below	60% - below	Study harder

LESSON 3

> Tell me and I'll forget. Show me, and I may remember. Involve me, and I'll understand.
>
> — Benjamin Franklin

Education

LESSON 3

GETTING THE PICTURE: Discuss the following questions in groups of three. Answer in complete sentences.

1. What is your fondest memory of school? Who was your best teacher? Why?

2. Discuss the levels of education in your country (pre-school, grade school, high school, etc). How are they similar to/different from those of the U.S. or Canada?

	YOUR COUNTRY																					
AGE	6	7	8	9	10	11	12	13	14	15	16	17	18	19	20	21	22	23	24	25	26	27
GRADE	1	2	3	4	5	6	7	8	9	10	11	12										
THE U.S.	Elementary School						Junior High School		Senior High School (High School Diploma)				University/College Undergraduate (Bachelor)				University/College Graduate (Masters) (Ph.D.)				Postdoctoral Study and Research	
							Middle School		High School (High School Diploma)				Junior/Community College (Associate)				Professional School					
									Vocational High School (High School Diploma)													
CANADA (British Columbia)	Elementary School						Secondary School (Diploma)						University/College Undergraduate (Bachelor)				University/College Graduate (Masters) (Doctorate)				Postdoctoral Study and Research	
													Junior/Community College (Associate)				Professional School					

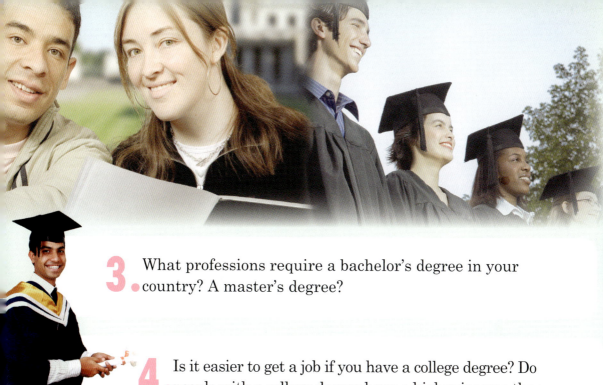

3. What professions require a bachelor's degree in your country? A master's degree?

4. Is it easier to get a job if you have a college degree? Do people with a college degree have a higher income than those without one?

5. What is your profession? Is it related to your education? Do you know anyone whose job is not related to his/her degree? (example: a nurse working as an administrative assistant)

6. In your country, at what stage do you start learning English? How is it different from your experience learning English at Zoni?

Jigsaw

A. READING: ANALYZING ADVERTISEMENTS

Work in groups and select an ad. Identify the idioms in each and figure out their meanings based on contextual clues. Then answer the questions. Explain your idioms to the other groups.

1. Describe the picture. What do you think the picture conveys?

2. According to the ad, what does **pass with flying colors** mean?

3. What do you think an *Ivy League* school is? Do you know any **Ivy League** schools?

4. In your own opinion, is studying English **as easy as ABC**?

> **Do you want to pass with flying colors and enter an Ivy League school?**
>
> It's as easy as ABC. Enroll at Zoni Inc.! Ace your way into college by enrolling in our TOEFL iBT, IELTS, ACT, PSAT, SAT, AP, and CLEP test preparation courses.
>
> We have flexible schedules and affordable prices. Visit www.zoni.com for more details or call 212-555-1212 and speak to a student service representative.
>
> **ZONI: your road to success!!!**

1. Have you ever joined a book club?

2. What do members do during club meetings?

3. What does **bookworm** mean? Describe someone you know who is a bookworm.

> **Calling all bookworms!**
>
> Come join our book club. Get to share your insights about your favorite books or read your favorite poems aloud. Get the latest news about upcoming novels and book readings by your favorite authors. Club meetings are held at Rosendale Hall every Friday at 3:30 p.m. Complimentary coffee and pastries are provided. Bring a friend with you. The more the merrier!☺

Working your way through college?

Get financial aid or a scholarship. Visit **www.studyfree.com** to apply for scholarship programs or receive information about financial assistance.

Start early! Application deadlines are 9 to 12 months before the semester begins.

You no longer need to worry about tuition fees. All you have to do is hit the books, put on your thinking caps and think about your future...

1. What does it mean to **work your way through college**? Is this common in your country?

2. Are the phrases **hit the books** and **put on your thinking caps** used literally in the ad? What do they mean?

Lina is such a smart cookie. What's her secret?

VITALIX MULTIVITAMINS:
Boost your memory and learn in a snap.

Made from natural ingredients such as gingko biloba, ginseng and rosemary, it is doctor recommended. It's also formulated to meet the daily recommended allowance of vitamins and minerals needed for longevity.

So what are you waiting for? Be on the honor roll or be the teacher's pet with the help of Vitalix multivitamins.

Now available at pharmacies and supermarkets.

1. Why do you think Lina is such a **smart cookie**?

2. What does Vitalix multivitamins do to one's body?

3. Do you think that taking multivitamins will guarantee you **being on the honor roll**?

4. Do you think Lina is a **teacher's pet**? Are you a teacher's pet?

B. DISCOVER THE MEANING

Match the sentences in column A with the sentences in column B to create short dialogues. Write the letter in the blanks provided and compare your answers with your partner.

COLUMN A	COLUMN B
___ 1. **Kyra:** I really have to study hard so I can *pass the course with flying colors*.	**A. Ben:** Why were you the teacher's favorite student? Did you get a lot of A's?
___ 2. **Tom:** I intend to go to an *Ivy League* school too. Most of my family graduated from Harvard University.	**B. Bong-Ku:** Well, if you want to be on the list of students with exceptional achievements, you'd better study extra hard.
___ 3. **Takashi:** I don't know why Dad is having such a hard time learning to use a computer. It's *as easy as ABC*.	**C. Marcel:** Wow, I admire you! You work very hard to pay for your college expenses.
___ 4. **Mujgan:** I love being independent, but I have to *work my way through* college. I stopped asking my parents for financial help a year ago.	**D. Mom:** Honey, it may be very easy for you but your dad comes from an older generation. Maybe you should help him learn faster.

___ **5. Teresa:** Thanks for the invitation, but I really have to *hit the books*. My midterms are next week.

___ **6. Ms. Torres:** Ok, class! This question is worth 10 points so you need to *put your thinking caps on* in order to get it right.

___ **7. Luisa:** Aurora is a *smart cookie*. I wish I had her brains.

___ **8. Feng:** In my school days, I was the *teacher's pet*. My classmates hated me for that.

___ **9. Kyung-Li:** I want to be on the *honor roll*. My dad will give me a Porsche if I make it.

___ **10. Jon:** I know what to give Cecilia for her birthday. Since she's a *bookworm*, I'm giving her the collected poems of Emily Dickinson.

E. Chandra: I know. She's a very clever person. Everybody would like to be like her.

F. Sung: Are you sure? You have plenty of time to begin studying hard. Come on! You need to have some fun!

G. Student: Oh no! I fell asleep last night and forgot to read the chapter. I need to think really hard and give an answer.

H. Mehmet: That's a great idea! She'll love your present because she likes to read a lot. I think I'll get her a novel.

I. Mr. Perez: Have you thought about going to Yale or Princeton instead? They are also famous universities here in the U.S.

J. John: Can I join you? I want to get a good grade in that class, too.

Practice

A. Read the statements below and complete them with the appropriate idiom from the list. Use the correct verb form. Then circle AGREE if you agree with the statement or DISAGREE if you disagree. You may use each idiom only once. Compare your answers with a partner.

bookworm	work your way through college	honor roll
smart cookie	as easy as ABC	hit the books
learn in a snap	Ivy League	teacher's pet

1. If you go to an _____ school, you will get the best education in the world.

    ☐ AGREE ☐ DISAGREE

2. An English-English dictionary will help you _____ the language _____.

    ☐ AGREE ☐ DISAGREE

3. It's a compliment to be called a _____.

    ☐ AGREE ☐ DISAGREE

4. Learning a second language is _____.

☐ **AGREE** ☐ **DISAGREE**

5. Being a _____ is hereditary.

☐ **AGREE** ☐ **DISAGREE**

6. If you are a _____, you have an extensive vocabulary.

☐ **AGREE** ☐ **DISAGREE**

7. Being on the _____ makes a person popular.

☐ **AGREE** ☐ **DISAGREE**

8. If you _____ a week before your exams, you will pass with flying colors.

☐ **AGREE** ☐ **DISAGREE**

9. _____ is not easy but it makes you feel proud of yourself.

☐ **AGREE** ☐ **DISAGREE**

B. GUESS THE IDIOM: Pick one idiom from the list. You can also use idioms from previous lessons. Act it out or draw it on the board. Your classmates will guess your idiom. Ask one of your classmates to use the idiom in his/her own sentence.

Let's break the ice!

ADVERB CLAUSES OF TIME

A. On a small piece of paper, complete the sentences below about yourself. Don't write your name on the paper and do not show it to anyone! Let's see who among your classmates can figure out who you are.

I am studying at Zoni while I am...
I have... since...
I will... until...
I get nervous whenever I...
I lived in... before I came

Now fold your paper and give it to your teacher.

ADVERB CLAUSES OF TIME

There are many time expressions that you can use in adverb clauses of time. Look at the examples below and figure out the meaning of each time expression by working on the exercise below this table.

when	• My sister was working on her thesis **when her computer crashed**. • I had completed my master's degree **when I got the job**. • My brother looked for a better job **when his first son was born**. • I will call you **when I get home**.

before	• I had paid my tuition fee **before my uncle offered to help**. • Becky will prepare dinner **before she studies for her exam**.
after	• My uncle offered help **after I had paid my tuition**. • Becky will study **after she prepares dinner**.
while as	• He called **while I was working on my research paper**. • Marcela came **as I was leaving the house**.
by the time	• I had already taken my TOEFL exam **by the time the university replied to my application**. • I will have done my homework **by the time you finish work**.
until	• He will continue to study **until he completes his doctorate**. • My parents worked very hard **until my siblings and I graduated from college**.
since	• He has worked in that company **since he was 18 years old**. • I haven't seen my family **since I came here 3 years ago**.
as soon as	• I will call you **as soon as I get to the airport**. • I will start looking for a job **as soon as I finish college**.
every time whenever	• She gets nervous **whenever she has an exam**. • Lisa blushes **every time she speaks in front of a crowd**.
the first (second, next, last etc.) time	• **The first time I visited the US**, I was amazed. • **I still cried the second time** I saw that movie.
as long as	• You will be my best friend **as long as I live**. • We should study at Zoni **as long as we can**.

B. VOCABULARY PRACTICE: Look at the examples in the previous page. With your partner, find out the meaning of each adverb of time based on the way it is used in the sentences. Write the letter of your answers before each number.

COLUMN A	COLUMN B
___ 1. by the time	a. specific chronological point
___ 2. as soon as	b. prior
___ 3. whenever/every time	c. subsequent
___ 4. after	d. during that time
___ 5. since	e. one event or action is completed before another one
___ 6. while/as	f. up to that time
___ 7. when	g. from that time
___ 8. until	h. right after something else happens
___ 9. before	i. each time
___ 10. the first/second/last time	j. that particular time
___ 11. as long as	k. for the duration

C. Circle the appropriate time expression for each sentence below.

1. I love going to Bryant Park in New York! I take my laptop _____ I go there because there's free Internet connection.

   a. as soon as   b. every time   c. while   d. until

2. Debbie had completed 2 college degrees _____ she got married.

    a. before   **b.** whenever   **c.** as soon as   **d.** when

3. Jerry will work in this company _____ he retires.

    a. the last time   **b.** as soon as   **c.** whenever   **d.** until

4. He offered to help me with my homework _____ I had done it.

    a. every time   **b.** before   **c.** after   **d.** while

5. We saw Mr. Duffey _____ we were leaving the house.

    a. whenever   **b.** as   **c.** after   **d.** before

6. The Simpsons will purchase a house _____ they inherit millions from their parents.

    a. every time   **b.** until   **c.** by the time   **d.** as soon as

7. I know the TOEFL test can be very challenging but don't worry. We can take it again and again _____ we get the right score for college admission.

    a. until   **b.** by the time   **c.** after   **d.** as soon as

8. My daughter didn't eat _____ I came home.

    a. whenever   **b.** as   **c.** until   **d.** the next time

9. Elizabeth was watching the news _____ she saw me on TV.

    a. every time   **b.** as soon as   **c.** when   **d.** while

10. I will never give up _____ I speak English very well!

    a. by the time   **b.** when   **c.** as soon as   **d.** until

D. Work in groups of three and write the correct tense of the verbs below in parentheses. If you are not sure, you may refer to the examples above.

1. I had seen snow before I _____ **(go)** to New York.

2. As soon as Henry _____ **(get)** to the airport, he will call you.

3. Mary and John _____ **(know)** each other since they were in grade school.

4. Husband: "I promise. I _____ **(stay)** with you until I find a rich woman."

    Wife: "Oh, Bob. Are you _____ **(look for)** a divorce?"

5. Student 1: "Hey, you look like you didn't get a good night's sleep."

   Student 2: "Yeah. I _____ (not, go) to bed until I had finished my research paper.

6. My brother _____ (come) to New Jersey whenever my mother _____ (want) to see him.

7. Yesterday, while I was walking on 34th street, I _____ (see) my high school friend.

8. Evelin went to the Empire State Building the first time she _____ (visit) New York.

9. I'm telling you. By the time Rey completes his college degree, he _____ (have) about 10 girlfriends.

10. By the time I finish all my courses at Zoni Language Centers, I _____ (meet) hundreds of people from different countries. It will be my best experience ever!

Party Time

Stand up and interview your classmates using the questions below.
The first student to finish the interview is the winner.

Questions	Name	Answers
Ex. (SINCE) How long have you studied English?	Maria	Maria has studied English since she was in grade school.
1. (UNTIL) How long will you stay in this country?		
2. (THE FIRST TIME) Where did you travel the first time you took a plane flight?		
3. (AS SOON AS) What will you do once the class is over?		
4. (BEFORE) When did you come to this country?		
5. (WHEN) When will you visit your country?		

6. (WHENEVER) How do you prepare for an exam?		
7. (SINCE) How long have you been speaking English?		
8. (AS LONG AS) How long will I be your friend?		

Homework

Complete the sentences with your own information. Report your sentences to the class.

1. We should keep on studying until _____.

2. I will study English as long as _____.

3. I always _____ whenever I'm stressed out.

4. I _____ the first time I came to this school.

5. My best friend will _____ as soon as he/she _____.

Communicating Effectively

A. JIGSAW: When is it difficult to understand a person you're talking to? With your group, list as many answers as you can.

1. When he or she has a very strong accent.
2. When there is a lot of background noise.
3. _____.
4. _____.
5. _____.
6. _____.
7. _____.
8. _____.
9. _____.
10. _____.

B. Now listen to your teacher speak. Pretend you don't understand. What will you tell him/her?

_____
_____
_____
_____

C. Read the suggestions below and practice them with a partner.

FORMAL	INFORMAL
I'm sorry?	I'm sorry, I didn't catch that.
Excuse me?	What?
Pardon me?	Huh?
Come again, please!	
Excuse me? What was that again?	
Sorry, could you repeat that again please?	
Would you mind speaking a bit more slowly?	

Lights, Camera, Action!

ROLE PLAY: Work in pairs. Prepare a dialogue using the adverb clauses of time. Pretend that one of you doesn't understand the other. Use the examples in the table above or one of the strategies in your list. Role-play your dialogue in class.

Example: **A:** How long will you work at your current job?

B: I will work there until the end of time.

A: I'm sorry, could you say that again? It's very noisy here.

B: Sure, I will work until the end of time.

Practice! Then... perform!

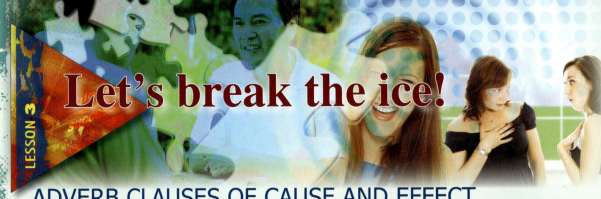

Let's break the ice!

ADVERB CLAUSES OF CAUSE AND EFFECT

In groups of three, answer the questions below using the words in parentheses. Each member of the group must answer in complete sentences. Present your answers to the class.

1. Why are some people never satisfied with their lives? **(Because)**

2. What are you able to do better now that you can speak English better? **(Now that)**

3. Why do parents want their children to learn their native language even if they live in an English-speaking country? **(Since)**

ADVERB CLAUSES OF CAUSE & EFFECT

These adverb clauses are used to explain the reasons why something happens. In the example below, you will see a popular way of expressing reason using BECAUSE.

Example: I study hard **because I want to land a good job**.

Now let's look at cue words used in explaining reasons:

because	**Example:** Patricia chose to study at Union County College *because* **it is close to her apartment**. • The adverb clause in this sentence explains why Patricia chose Union County College.

PAGE 90   ZONI LANGUAGE CENTERS ©

since	**Examples:** *Since* **computers are so much in-demand nowadays,** Jose decided to take some programming courses at NYU. Most parents send their kids to public schools *since* **private schools can be extremely expensive.** • *Since* is like *because*.
due to the fact that **in as much as**	**Examples:** The unemployment rate is climbing *due to the fact that* **most companies outsource their jobs to other countries.** The unemployment rate is climbing *in as much as* **most companies outsource their jobs to other countries.** • You may notice here that *due to the fact* & *in as much as* are like *since*. The difference is that they are very formal and usually used in written form.
now that	**Example:** *Now that* **I have a full-time job,** I can apply for health insurance soon. • If we break down the sentence to get to its meaning, it will be: *I can apply for health insurance soon because I have a job now.*

Pair Practice

Combine the two sentences using the words in parentheses below.
Compare your answers with your partner.

1. My father is sick. He didn't go to work. **(because)**

_____

2. I have a brand new car. I can go anywhere I want.
(now that)

_____

3. He didn't study hard in high school. It's very hard for him to be admitted to college. **(since)**

_____

4. Pollution on Earth is getting worse. A lot of people are getting sick. **(due to the fact that)**

_____

5. Thanksgiving is a holiday. Our school is closed.
(since)

_____

6. Jessie doesn't drink alcohol. He's allergic to it.
(because)

_____

7. John and Carol have a house with a huge backyard. They are going to plant vegetables. **(now that)**

_____

8. Melissa is having a difficult time looking for a new job. A lot of companies are laying off employees. **(in as much as)**

_____

9. The snowstorm has stopped. We can drive to Pennsylvania. **(now that)**

_____

10. Teachers are encouraged to pursue a master's degree. It is a requirement if they want to teach at colleges and universities. **(due to the fact that)**

_____

Group Work

In groups of three, complete the sentences below. Report your sentences to the class.

1. Now that I live in _____, _____.

2. Since our vacation is coming up, we _____.

3. _____ due to the fact that education is important.

4. Some people aren't successful because _____.

ZONI LANGUAGE CENTERS ©

Round Robin Story

⏳ 5 min. Work in groups of four and make up a one-paragraph story using as many adverb clauses of time and adverb clauses showing cause and effect as possible. Each member must contribute ideas. Assign a member of the group to write down the story. The group with the most correctly used adverb clauses wins.

USE: when, before, after, while/as, by the time, until, since, as soon as, every time/whenever, as long as...

Example:

My sister was working on her thesis when her computer crashed. Before I even asked her what I could do to help, she had already knocked the computer to the floor. She was sobbing because her entire work...

LEND ME YOUR EARS!

Literacy is traditionally defined as the ability to read and write. It gives people access to higher education and increases job opportunities. At present, many countries still face the problem of illiteracy and steps are being taken to address this social predicament. Building more schools, providing tutoring services and offering free education are just some of the solutions. Let's take a look at the world's literacy rates and answer the questions that follow.

See Teacher's Manual

Listen to your teacher carefully and circle the correct answers below.

1. Illiteracy is a condition that can be changed if you go to school.

    a: ☐ True   **b:** ☐ False

2. 1/5 of the world's population was illiterate in 1998.

    a: ☐ True   **b:** ☐ False

3. More men were illiterate than women in the Arab states as of 2006.

    a: ☐ True   **b:** ☐ False

4. More than half of India's population is illiterate.

    a: ☐ True   **b:** ☐ False

5. Latin America has the same literacy rate as the United States.

    a: ☐ True   **b:** ☐ False

6. What does the statement imply?

    a: ☐ Adults who are functionally illiterate cannot get a job.

    b: ☐ Adults who are functionally illiterate can earn as much as doctors and lawyers.

    c: ☐ Adults who are functionally illiterate don't have a difficult time keeping their jobs.

    d: ☐ None of the above.

Conversation Practice

Student A: Read the questions to Student B.
Student B: Close your book. Listen carefully to Student A. Use the conversation strategies you learned from this unit if you don't understand student A's questions.

When done, switch roles. Student B will now ask student A questions. Use the sample dialogue below as a model.

Example:

Student A: Why is it good to be a bookworm?

Student B: I'm sorry? Could you say that again?

Student A: Why is it good to be a bookworm?

Student B: Oh, I think it's good to be a bookworm because it helps a person expand his or her vocabulary.

Student A

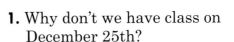

Questions

1. Why don't we have class on December 25th?

2. Is it good to be a teacher's pet?

3. What do you usually do whenever you feel anxious about your future?

4. How long will you study here?

Answers: 1. As soon as 2. Because 3. Since 4. As long as

Student B

Questions

1. When will you get married?

2. Why is it beneficial to be on the honor roll?

3. Why do some people go to the gym?

4. How long will I stay your friend?

Answers: 1. Due to the fact   2. Because   3. Whenever   4. Until

Drawing

Draw three things that you are still dreaming of becoming: (example: a popular singer, a famous inventor, a school owner, etc.) Share your work with the class and explain your dreams.

Homework

In one or two paragraphs, write why you dream of the three things you drew on page 97. Do you still plan to pursue them? If not, explain what caused you to stop "dreaming." If yes, how do you plan to achieve your dreams? What are your alternative plans? Use adverb clauses of time and cause and effect in your composition. Read your composition to the class.

My Dream

Be a Detective

Underline and correct the errors in the sentences below. There could be more than one error in each item.

Ex: Don't worry. He will love you as long as he ~~live~~ *lives*.

1. My parents will meet us when we will have arrived at the airport.

2. I intend to go back to my country as soon as I will finish my English studies.

3. Because I came to New York, I pictured it as an exciting city with a lot of honest and well-mannered people. Now this I'm here, my perception has changed.

4. She wants to taught a kindergarten class since she'll love working with younger children.

5. He gets cold feet as long as he sees her in the cafeteria.

Let's Debate!

Form two groups and debate one of the topics below in class.

- It is important to graduate from a well-known university
- Parents must send their children to a good private school
- Sex education must be taught in high school

Let's Google it!

Choose one of the three topics below for your internet research. Report your interesting findings to the class.

Suggested topics:
- Steps in applying to colleges/universities in the U.S./Canada
- Inclusion of sex education in grade school and high school curricula
- Public schools versus private schools

Quiz Yourself!

A. Choose the correct answers and write them in the blanks provided.

1. _____ the test is difficult, you had better get some sleep.

    a. As soon as   **b.** Since   **c.** As

2. _____ he loves music so much, he decided to go to a conservatory.

    a. Because   **b.** Though   **c.** When

3. They won't be able to buy any properties _____ they don't have enough money.

    a. because   **b.** whether or not   **c.** as long as

4. We waited _____ he finished his work, then we hung out for a couple of hours.

    a. although   **b.** before   **c.** until

5. We will have finished our dinner _____ they arrive from the opera.

    a. by   **b.** by the time   **c.** as

6. They received high marks on their exams _____ they had studied very hard.

    a. because   **b.** as soon as   **c.** whereas

7. She went to bed _____ I had left.

    a. until   **b.** after   **c.** by the time

8. I have played the flute _____ I was a young boy.

    a. as long as   **b.** since   **c.** because

9. _____ you need me, I'll be asleep.

    a. In case   **b.** As   **c.** By the time

10. I saw Danny _____ I went to San Diego.

    a. even though   **b.** the last time   **c.** as long as

11. We will be working long hours for an extra week _____ we have not yet finished.

    a. due to the fact that   **b.** though   **c.** as long as

12. We go hiking and camping _____ he visits.

    a. because   **b.** every time   **c.** whereas

13. My uncle has been teaching English _____ I was in high school.

    a. as soon as   **b.** whenever   **c.** since

14. _____ I saw you, I fell in love right away.

    a. As long as   **b.** By the time   **c.** The first time

B. IDIOMS: Circle the best answer to complete the dialogue.

1. A: I'm so impressed with Sandra. She has a very extensive vocabulary.

B: _____

    a. That's because she's a bookworm.

    b. That's because she's a teacher's pet.

2. A: _____

B: I'm really proud of you, son.

    a. Dad, I've decided to work my way through college. I found a well-paying job.

    b. Dad, I don't think I'll pass my exams with flying colors.

3. A: My daughter is on the honor roll!

B: _____

    a. She must go to an Ivy League school.

    b. She must be a smart cookie like you.

4. A: _____

B: Well, it's not that easy for me to learn it, so I have to study harder and practice more.

    a. Learning English as a second language is not as easy as ABC.
    b. Learning English as a second language is as easy as ABC.

5. A: How did you manage to know all the answers in the test?

B: _____

    a. I hit the books every day, so the test was a piece of cake.
    b. I work my way through college so it was a piece of cake.

6. A: Why is it so expensive to study at Harvard?

B: _____

    a. It's because you don't have to work your way through college.
    b. It's because it is an Ivy League school, and they have the best professors.

Check your answers with the class. Count your points and check your score.

POINTS	PERCENTAGE	POINTS
18-20	90% - 100%	Great job!
15-17	75% - 85%	Very good!
13 - 14	65% - 70%	Good!
12 and below	60% - below	Study harder

LESSON 4

> Choose a job you love, and you will never have to work a day in your life.
>
> *Confucius*

LESSON 4: Career

WARM-UP (GAME): WHAT DO I DO FOR A LIVING?
Work in groups of three or four and complete the crossword below. No dictionaries are allowed. Chances are, there will be two or more words that you may not be able to figure out. Assign a leader for your group and wait for your teacher's instruction on when each leader should move from one group to another until your puzzle is complete.

See Teacher's Manual

ACROSS

1. a person who maintains and audits company accounts
6. a person who repairs machines or devices
7. a person trained to compete in a sport
8. an administrative position responsible for receiving visitors and answering the telephone
9. a person who writes articles, stories, or books
10. a manager or a supervisor, usually in very high position in a business organization
11. a real estate agent or broker
13. a person hired to carry luggage and supplies
17. a person who plays or composes music

DOWN

2. a person who makes and fits eyeglasses
3. a person responsible for determining the final content of a text, such as for a newspaper, magazine or book
4. a person hired to take care of a property or a person
5. a person who works for the government
9. a person who plans and designs buildings
12. a person who makes and alters garments
14. someone who is running for government office or has already won an election and holds an office
15. a person who operates an aircraft
16. a college university teacher, not a professor yet
18. a person who makes or sells jewelry
19. a public official who decides cases in court

PAGE 106 ZONI LANGUAGE CENTERS ©

Please complete the crossword puzzle below

Jigsaw

In groups of three or four, fill in the table below with the jobs that apply in each category. List as many jobs in each column as you can. Report your findings to the class.

JOBS THAT DO NOT REQUIRE FORMAL EDUCATION	**Ex:** sanitation worker
JOBS THAT REQUIRE AT LEAST A HIGH SCHOOL DEGREE	
JOBS YOU CAN GET WITH AN ASSOCIATE'S DEGREE	
JOBS THAT REQUIRE A BACHELOR'S DEGREE	
JOBS THAT REQUIRE A MASTER'S / DOCTORAL DEGREE	

Getting The Picture

Discuss the following questions with two group mates. Then report your answers to the class.

1. Describe your first job. Did you like it? How did you find the job? Was it related to your skills and education?

2. How would you rank the following from the most to the least important: position, salary, boss, popularity of the organization, location, co-workers, benefits, work environment, work schedule? Rank the items individually, then discuss the results in your group.

3. Would you prefer to be an employee with a stable income or a businessperson with an unpredictable income?

4. If you could own your own business, what would it be? Why? Where would it be located? Describe the services/products you would offer. How big would you want your business to be?

5. Describe an ideal boss/supervisor.

6. What are some good reasons to quit a job? To keep a job?

7. What are some good reasons to terminate an employee?

A. READING: Work in groups of three. Underline new vocabulary and use an English dictionary to look up the meanings. Report your findings to the other groups.

Ten Tips on Preparing for a Job Interview

Your hard work has finally paid off. After sending out all those cover letters and résumés, you've been called in for a face-to-face job interview. However, it is not yet time to sit back, relax and dream about how you are going to spend your salary. There is still a lot of work to do. Keep in mind that there are dozens of other highly qualified candidates going after your job. It's very important for you to stand out from the others. A job interview is similar to a social conversation, but you will have to "sell" yourself to a prospective employer during that crucial first meeting.

Here are 10 important tips to help you in your interview, which will hopefully lead to your next job:

1 **Do your homework.** Do some research about the company prior to the interview so that you can showcase that knowledge during the meeting. This will boost your credibility and will help you formulate intelligent questions to ask the interviewer.

2 **Know where you're going.** Make sure to find out where the office is and how to get there. You should know how long the trip will take and the name and phone number of the person you will be meeting with.

3 **Dress for success.** You need to look the part; therefore, you have to dress appropriately. There is only one chance to make a good first impression. Your clothing should be neat, pressed, and professional looking. Also, make sure to have a neat haircut and clean, manicured nails.

4 **Rehearse beforehand.** Prior to your interview, prepare answers to common questions the interviewer is likely to ask, such as *What are your strengths and weaknesses? Why do you want to work here? Why should we hire you? What can you contribute to the company?* and *Tell me about yourself.* Conduct a mock interview with a trusted friend for practice.

5 **Secure your references.** Find at least three people, such as former supervisors, colleagues, or instructors, who are willing to serve as your professional references. Be sure to get their permission beforehand, and be certain that they will speak highly of you if contacted by a potential employer.

6 **Allow sufficient time for the interview.** Be sure to arrive at least 15 minutes before the interview. There is no excuse for tardiness. Visit the restroom and check your appearance in the mirror. Inform the receptionist that you have arrived and that you have an appointment. Turn your cell phone or any noise-making devices off so they don't ring during your meeting.

7 **Bring necessary documentation.** Bring important documents such as extra copies of your résumé, a passport, driver's license, Social Security card, or portfolio of writing samples or other professional work.

8 **Sell yourself.** The interview is your chance to shine. First, you must establish a rapport with the interviewer, then follow his or her leads. Respond to questions being asked. Stress your achievements, your strengths, your abilities, and what sets you uniquely apart from other applicants. Talk about why you are interested in the position and what you can offer the company.

9 **Be prepared to ask questions.** Insightful questions allow the interviewer to evaluate your personal and professional needs. You may also inquire about salary, vacation, retirement and benefits.

10 **Follow up.** After the interview, don't forget to thank the interviewer for his or her time and consideration. Restate your interest and commitment to the position. Tell the employer how much you would enjoy working for the company. If you don't hear anything after one week, call to politely inquire when they will be making a final decision.

Every interview is a valuable learning experience. You may get the job that has been offered to you or you may not. In case you don't get the job, just look on the brighter side. You'll be more prepared and more at ease with the whole process for the next job interview. And remember that having a positive frame of mind is always helpful.

B. VOCABULARY PRACTICE

Match the words with their definitions and/or synonyms by using contextual clues (figuring out the meaning of the word by the way it is used in a sentence). Write the corresponding letter in the blanks provided.

COLUMN A	COLUMN B
___ 1. pay off	a. to exhibit, especially in an attractive or favorable aspect
___ 2. stand out	b. important or essential
___ 3. prospective	c. increase
___ 4. crucial	d. likely to be or become
___ 5. showcase	e. trustworthiness
___ 6. boost	f. relation marked by harmony, conformity, accord
___ 7. credibility	g. a selection of professional work compiled over a period of time and used for assessing performance or progress
___ 8. portfolio	h. to be beneficial or profitable
___ 9. rapport	i. to practice a set routine or performance
___ 10. rehearse	j. to be distinctive or prominent

C. READING COMPREHENSION:
Work in groups of three. Answer the questions below based on the previous reading activity.

1. What are the common questions asked in a job interview?

2. Why is it advisable to conduct a mock interview?

3. From whom can you secure references for your job interview?

4. Why is dressing up and establishing rapport important?

5. How can you "sell yourself" during a job interview?

6. What kind of documents should you bring to a job interview?

D. HOMEWORK: Choose five words from the vocabulary list and use them in your own sentences. Report your sentences to the class.

Impressive!

Example:

portfolio – The manager was very impressed with the applicant's portfolio.

1. _____ – _____

2. _____ – _____

3. _____ – _____

4. _____ – _____

5. _____ – _____

ADVERB CLAUSES OF CONTRAST
Let's Break The Ice

LESSON 4

Look at the two pictures and come up with a sentence using the provided time indicator.

 whereas

Ex.

Rosa dresses too casually, **whereas** the other workers dress professionally.

 because

1. Mr. Smith (be sad) (be laid off)

 even though

2. Mr. Philip (come to work) (has a headache)

 whereas

3. Mrs. Mendez (work at a law firm) Mr. Mendez (work at a construction site)

ZONI LANGUAGE CENTERS ©

ADVERB CLAUSES OF CONTRAST

In this table, we will see sentences that express opposition and unexpected results.

Because	• **Because** the boss seemed unfriendly, I didn't take the job. • **Because** this job is closer to my house, I won't take the other, higher paying job.
Even though **Although** **Though**	• **Even though** being a nurse is difficult, Ruby enjoys her job a lot. • **Although** Albert was promoted, his salary did not increase. • **Though** I work out at the gym, I still gain weight easily.
While **Whereas**	• My daughter is very talkative, **while** my son is very quiet. • Some people prefer easy jobs, **whereas** others enjoy challenging positions. **Note:** Whereas is more formal and usually used in written form.

Pair Practice

Fill in the blanks with **Even though**, **Because**, or **While/Whereas**:

1. _____ her parents couldn't afford it, Duygu was not able to fulfill her dream of completing her degree in London.

2. Your job is very exciting, _____ mine is really boring.

3. The new receptionist is really pleasant, _____ the other one is very rude.

4. John quit his job _____ he knew he was going to get fired anyway.

5. _____ Jonas works very hard, he can't seem to earn enough to pay all his bills.

6. Sheila won the competition _____ she didn't sing very well.

7. Teachers in the U.S. receive a lot of benefits, _____ teachers in other countries do not get paid enough.

8. _____ it was very difficult, Mary had to leave her country to work and be able to provide for her 5 children.

9. _____ you were terminated due to insubordination, it will be hard for you to look for another job.

10. Henry pursued his career in law _____ a lot of people discouraged him from doing so.

Homework

Complete the sentences below based on your personal experience.
Share your answers in group tomorrow!

1. I am _____, **whereas** + brother/sister is _____

   I always wore hand-me-downs from my older sister, whereas she always got new clothes.

2. **Because** _____, I didn't _____.

3. I will _____ **even though** _____

Let's Talk

SPEAKING PRACTICE: With a partner, answer the questions below using the words in parentheses. Strictly no writing. Speaking only!

1. Why is it beneficial to have a master's degree? **(because)**

2. Which would you prefer: being an employee or having your own business? Why? **(whereas)**

3. It's hard to live in a different culture. Do you want to live here for good? **(even though)**

4. Why is it important to have a bachelor's degree? **(because)**

5. Sometimes, it's hard to get up in the morning and go to work. What do you do in such situations? **(even though)**

6. Lawyer or doctor? Which would you prefer to be? Why? **(while)**

Communicating Effectively
EXPRESSING, ACCEPTING & REJECTING IDEAS

A. Practice the dialogue below in groups of three.

Mary: "Hey guys! I'm looking for a job. What would be an easy and high-paying job?"

Pete: "It seems to me that there's no such thing as an easy job."

Mary: "That's true. I never heard of anyone not complaining about their work."

Danny: "I'm not sure I agree with you guys. I am happy with my job. In fact, I'm not paid well enough, but I like what I'm doing."

B. In the dialogue you read, who first expressed an idea/opinion? Who accepted the idea? Who rejected it? Share your answers within your group.

In the same group, change the three underlined groups of words into other possible ways of expressing, accepting and rejecting ideas. Then present the dialogue in class with your new conversation strategies.

C. Study the table below of different ways of expressing, accepting and rejecting ideas. Practice saying them using the right gestures and intonation.

Expressing ideas	Accepting ideas	Rejecting ideas
I think…	I think so/I think so, too.	I don't think so.
In my opinion…	I totally agree with you.	I'm afraid I disagree.
It seems to me that…	That's right/true.	Maybe, but…
Personally, I believe/think…	Exactly.	I can see what you mean but…
If you ask me, I'd say that…	You're absolutely right.	I see your point but…
I'm pretty sure that…	You have a point there.	I'm sorry but I don't see it the same way.
	That's a good point.	
	You can say that again.	

PAGE 120   ZONI LANGUAGE CENTERS ©

D. In groups of three, answer the following questions by assigning roles to each member. One will express an idea, one will accept the idea and the third will reject it.

Question: Is it better to work abroad?

Student A: <u>I'd say that</u> it's best to work in your own country.

Student B: <u>I totally agree with you</u>. I don't see any point in going to another country just for work.

Student C: <u>I'm sorry but I don't see it the same way</u>. Some jobs pay more in other countries. That's why many people opt to work overseas.

Now refer to your table to practice the conversation strategies in expressing, accepting and rejecting ideas.

1. Should women work after getting married?

2. Which is more important for promoting a person at work: educational attainment or experience?

3. Is money the most important factor in choosing a job?

4. What do you think the most prestigious job is?

5. Which would you rather have: a high-paying but boring job or a low-paying but exciting job?

LESSON 4

What will make you change your mind?

ADVERB CLAUSES OF CONDITION

A. LET'S BREAK THE ICE: Complete the table below about yourself. On the left column, write five things that you don't want to do. On the right, write the conditions that will make you do them.

THINGS THAT YOU DON'T WANT TO DO	WHAT WILL MAKE YOU DO THEM
Examples: Clean windows on high-rise buildings	**Examples:** $1,000,000 dollars
Marry a lazy, jobless man/woman	the man/woman is a millionaire
1.	
2.	
3.	
4.	
5.	

ADVERB CLAUSES OF CONDITION

In groups of three, discuss the differences among the sentences below.

unless	My boss will never terminate me **unless** I make a major mistake.
if *See use of if in past on the bonus page!*	I will get a raise **if** I work hard.
whether or not	I respect my colleagues' opinions **whether or not** I agree with them.
even if	I will continue to work **even if** I have enough money to retire.
only if	I will work overtime **only if** I get paid time and a half.
in the event that **in case**	I will take my book to work **in the event that** I have free time. **(in case)**

B. Now go back to your previous activity (What Will Make You Change Your Mind?) and make sentences using the adverb clause of conditions in the table above. Write your complete sentences in the blanks below, then read them to the class!

Examples: I will clean windows on high-rise buildings only if I'm paid $1,000,000.

I won't marry a lazy, jobless man/woman unless he/she is a millionaire.

1. _____

2. _____

3. _____

Practice

Complete the sentences with your own words.

Examples:

We will look for a great job even if _it takes forever_.

Martha's husband will allow her to work only if _she doesn't work full time_.

1. You can find a job whether or not _____.

2. John is going to work tomorrow even if _____.

3. Please tell Hakan that he can call me in case _____.

4. Mariella will never leave this company unless _____.

5. I am absent from work only if _____.

6. You can be a lawyer only if _____.

7. A person can obtain a green card if _____.

8. You can't be a teacher unless _____.

9. We can work in a corporate setting whether or not _____.

10. John can't pay all his bills unless _____.

UNTRUE CONDITIONAL IN THE PAST

This type of conditional expresses untrue ideas or events in the past. We also use this form to express regrets about the past.

would have
If + had Past Perfect + **could have** + past participle of the verb
might have

Examples:

If I *had stayed* in my country, I *would have bought* a house.
(In reality: I didn't stay in my country, I didn't buy a house.)

Create your own sentence:
If I had stayed in my country, I _____.

If I *hadn't come* to Zoni, I *wouldn't have met* so many people from different countries.
(In reality: I came to Zoni and I met many people from different countries.)

Create your own sentence:
If I hadn't come to Zoni, I _____.

Now share your sentences with your partners.

Oral Practice

Student A reads the first five sentences and Student B responds with the past conditions orally. Then switch your roles from No. 6 to 10.

Examples:

We didn't know about the time, so we came late.

→ <u>If we had known about the time, we wouldn't have come late.</u>

1. Jasmin didn't take the job, so she didn't have money to spend.
   → _____

2. Ozkan didn't feel well, so he didn't show up at the meeting.
→ _____

3. Jin Joo forgot to buy flour, so she couldn't bake a cake for her client.
→ _____

4. Julio didn't drive, so he missed the conference.
→ _____

5. Milena got home late, so she missed her boss's call.
→ _____

Switch your roles.

6. Daniel didn't go to work yesterday, so he didn't get his paycheck.
→ _____

7. They left the party early, so they didn't get a souvenir.
→ _____

8. We saw a movie, so we didn't go to the barbecue.
→ _____

9. Giselle went to London, so she didn't attend her best friend's wedding.
→ _____

10. I was absent for a week, so I have a lot of homework to do.
→ _____

Practice

Complete the sentences below.

1. I would have become rich if _____

2. My life would have changed if _____

3. If I hadn't come to the US, I would have _____

4. If I hadn't quit my previous job, I could have _____

5. If my dad had married a celebrity, he would have married _____

Survey

Read the items below and check the ones that are applicable to you. Then interview your partner and check his/her preferences. After taking turns, share your partners' answers with other pairs. Based on your findings, discuss and advise each other about what types of jobs are appropriate for each one of you.

	Very important	Important	Not important
1. Job security			
2. Prestige			
3. Benefits and good salary			
4. Working with your mind			
5. Working with your hands			
6. Having a routine; doing the same thing every day			
7. Having a variety of things to do			
8. Using your creativity, imagination or talent			
9. Being your own boss			
10. Working with a lot of people			
11. Engaging in physical activity			

Three possible jobs for your partner: 1. _____

2. _____

3. _____

IDIOMS: Job Hunting

Work in groups of three and read the following ads. Take note of the idioms highlighted and figure out the meaning based on the contextual clues. Report to the class.

Do you want to make a living? Look at the ads below and choose the job that is right for you!

HELP WANTED GENERAL

ARC WELDERS AND CONSTRUCTION WORKERS

Part-time/Full-time positions available; willing to put in 10 hours a day 4 days a week. Excellent salary and benefits. Interested applicants should send their résumés to 39 Main St. Pleasant Valley, NJ 07395 or fax to 347-213-5678.

SECRETARY

Must have good typing skills and people skills. Bilingual is a plus. Part-time positions available. Clock in at 1:30 p.m. and clock out at 6:30 p.m. Mon.-Fri. and every other Sat. $10-15/hour, based on experience. Send résumés to wantedjobs@zoni.com

NURSE ASSISTANTS

Nurse Assistants Wanted!!!
Immediate positions available.

Put your valuable skills to work in hospitals and nursing homes. Health Care Associates offers:

- **A chance to create your own work schedule.** You may get off early or work the graveyard shift.
- **Competitive salary plus excellent benefits**
- **The support of a highly respected, professional organization**

Call Lauren for more information, 201-555-2616 or fax your résumé to 555-765-2441

IDIOM:	IDIOM:	IDIOM:
MEANING:	MEANING:	MEANING:
IDIOM:	IDIOM:	IDIOM:
MEANING:	MEANING:	MEANING:

CLASSIFIEDS/CAREERS

Zoni Voice — Issue 7 vol. 1

JOB LISTING BY AGENCY

WB Jobs

White-collar and blue-collar jobs available!!!

Seeking qualified individuals for the following positions:

SECURITY OFFICERS
F/T or P/T, experience preferred but not mandatory. Must be 21 or older. Women are encouraged to apply. $500/week

ENGLISH / SPANISH / PORTUGUESE LANGUAGE TEACHERS
Need native speakers with college background and 2 years experience. $35-40 an hour.

DIRECTOR OF PUBLIC RELATIONS
Must have college or graduate degree in Public Relations and/or work experience in the field. Strong written and verbal communication skills. English/Spanish speaker desirable. Up to $60,000 per annum

HOUSEKEEPERS
(WITH OR WITHOUT EXPERIENCE)
We offer health benefits; paid time off; mileage incentive program

Interested applicants must mail their résumés to WBJobs Agency 245 Grand Ave. Brooklyn, NY 11226 or call Maria at 718-555-3029 for more information.

Tired of being a couch potato? It's time to bring home the bacon! **GET YOUR CAREER IN GEAR...**

Wanted:

- **SCHOOL BUS DRIVERS**
Full-time / Part-time positions available. $15-18/hour. Must have NY driver's license.

- **FORK-LIFT OPERATORS**
F/T or P/T job; willing to work all 3 shifts. Excellent benefits; salary is based on experience and/or performance

- **TAXI DRIVERS**
Must be willing to work nights and afternoons; some Saturdays. Good driving record is a must. $10-12/hour

Interested applicants, call 215-555-0034 and ask for Mr. Johnson.

IDIOM: _____
MEANING: _____

IDIOM: _____
MEANING: _____

IDIOM: _____
MEANING: _____

IDIOM: _____
MEANING: _____

IDIOM: _____
MEANING: _____

IDIOM: _____
MEANING: _____

Discover The Meaning

Work with a partner. Figure out the meanings of the idioms below and circle the correct letters. Report your answers in class.

1. Alex: It's so hard to **make a living** these days! You need to have the right credentials to make lots of money.

Ben: I totally agree! That's the reason why I'm pursuing my master's degree next semester.

    a. live and spend money   b. to earn money
    c. get lots of money

2. Jake: When I grow up, I want to have a **white-collar job**, just like dad.

Mom: Your father will be very pleased to hear that, son.

    a. wear a shirt with a white collar
    b. a job having to do with a non-office work environment
    c. a job having to do with an office environment

3. Amanda had to **put in** an extra shift at the office to make up for her absences last week.

    a. begin   b. to work fast
    c. accumulate hours

4-5. Rumi: My boss reprimanded me because I forgot to **clock in** the other day.

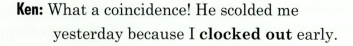

    a. use an alarm clock
    b. indicate specific time to start work
    c. complete hours at work

Ken: What a coincidence! He scolded me yesterday because I **clocked out** early.

    a. indicate specific time to finish work
    b. forgot to set the alarm
    c. do the time sheet

6. Blue-collar jobs such as postal delivery and factory work are decent jobs.

    a. to wear a blue uniform to work
    b. a job having to do with a non-office work environment
    c. a job that pays minimum wage

7. Joe: Hey Alison, let's call it a day! Do you want to go out for a drink?

Abdel: Sorry, I can't. I'm **getting off** work at 9:00 p.m. today. I have to finish the year-end report. How about a rain check?

    a. to leave work at the end of the workday
    b. to arrive in the office
    c. to go out with co-workers

8-9. Wife: Honey, you're turning into a **couch potato**! Our kids are growing up and both of us will have to **bring home the bacon**. You need to find a job.

Husband: Can't I just work from home?

couch potato:

  a. look like a potato
  b. someone who likes potatoes
  c. a person who spends a lot of time sitting or lying down, usually watching television

bring home the bacon:

  a. bring home a pack of bacon
  b. to earn a living, especially for a family
  c. have bacon for dinner

10. Dan: I don't get to see my roommate anymore. He's been working the **graveyard shift** since he landed that job.

Edwin: Wow! He must be exhausted when he gets home.

  a. cemetery job
  b. evening schedule
  c. morning schedule

Stand Up

Walk around the classroom and interview one another. Answer the questions below in complete sentences using the idioms and the correct verb tenses. Report your answers in class.

1. What do you do for a living? Do you enjoy it? Why or why not?

2. Why do most people prefer white-collar jobs to blue-collar jobs?

3. What are the advantages and disadvantages of working the graveyard shift?

4. How many hours per week do workers put in in your country? Is it the same in this country?

5. What do you usually do when you get off work?

6. Do you know anybody who is a couch potato? If yes, describe the person.

Pair Practice

Work in pairs and fill in the missing part of the idiom in each of the sentences below. Then practice the dialogue together and act it out in class.

George: I'm getting exhausted. Is it almost time to _____ out?

Jess: Are you kidding? We've only put _____ 5 hours of work.

George: That's it! I feel like we clocked _____ over 8 hours ago!

Jess: Stop complaining. Doing construction work is an excellent way to _____ a living.

George: I don't think so. I'd rather have a _____-collar job, just like my brother.

Jess: What does your brother do for a _____?

George: He's a paralegal in a prestigious law firm. He clocks in at 9:00 and gets _____ work at 6:00 p.m.

Jess: Does he always clock _____ at 6:00?

George: Not really, but he never has to work the graveyard _____ like we do!

Lights, Camera, Action!

ROLE PLAY: Work in pairs and create your own dialogue using the idioms on pages 130-132. Role-play your dialogue in front of the class.

See Teacher's Manual

Party Time

SCAVENGER HUNT: Walk around the classroom and interview your classmates based on the information below. If a classmate answers "yes," write his/her name in the blank next to the item. If a classmate answers "no," find another classmate until you get an affirmative answer. Get as many different names as possible. Ask appropriate questions based on the answers below. At the end, report your answers to the class.

Example:

Have you ever earned a living as a waitress?

____Carmen____ has made a living as a waitress.

1. Have you made a living as a waitress?

_____ has made a living as a waitress.

2. Would you like to work the graveyard shift?

_____ would like to work the graveyard shift.

3. Are you in charge of bringing home the bacon in the family?

_____ is in charge of bringing home the bacon in the family.

4. Did you use to be a couch potato?

_____ used to be a couch potato.

5. Did you get off work at 10:00 p.m. last night?

_____ got off work at 10:00 p.m. last night.

6. Do you need to clock in at 6:30 a.m.?

_____ needs to clock in at 6:30 a.m.

7. Did you put in 8 hours of work the day before yesterday?

_____ put in 8 hours of work the day before yesterday.

8. Would you rather have a blue-collar job than a white-collar job?

_____ would rather have a blue-collar job than a white-collar job.

Job Interview

Complete the application form below prior to your job interview.

APPLICATION FORM

Instructions: Type or print clearly in black or blue ink. Answer all questions.

NAME (Last, First, Middle)	SOC. SEC. #

ADDRESS (Number and Street, City, State, Zip Code)	PHONE NO.
	(_____) _____

POSITION DESIRED	☐ Full-time	☐ Part-time
	☐ Temporary	

DAYS/HOURS AVAILABLE

☐ Monday ☐ Tuesday ☐ Wednesday ☐ Thursday ☐ Friday ☐ Saturday ☐ Sunday

Hours Available: from _____ to _____

What date are you available to start work? *(mm/dd/yy)* _____ / _____ / _____

Have you worked for this company before?	☐ Yes	☐ No
Are you 18 or over?	☐ Yes	☐ No

EDUCATION

	NAME AND ADDRESS OF SCHOOL	MAJOR	DEGREE/ DIPLOMA
High School			
College			
Trade, business, other			

SPECIAL SKILLS AND QUALIFICATIONS: List job-related licenses, skills, training, honors, awards, and special accomplishments

EMPLOYMENT HISTORY: Start with present or most recent position

Employer:	
Address:	
Supervisor:	
Phone:	
Position Title:	
From: *(mm/dd/yy)* _____ / _____ / _____	**To:** *(mm/dd/yy)* _____ / _____ / _____
Duties:	
Salary:	first: $ _____ last: $ _____
Reason for leaving:	
Employer:	
Address:	
Supervisor:	
Phone:	
Position Title:	
From: *(mm/dd/yy)* _____ / _____ / _____	**To:** *(mm/dd/yy)* _____ / _____ / _____
Duties:	
Salary:	first: $ _____ last: $ _____
Reason for leaving:	

May we contact your present employer? ☐ Yes ☐ No

REFERENCES: Exclude relatives

	Name/Title	Address and Phone No.	Occupation
1.			
2.			
3.			

I CERTIFY THAT THE INFORMATION CONTAINED IN THIS APPLICATION IS TRUE AND COMPLETE TO THE BEST OF MY KNOWLEDGE AND UNDERSTAND THAT ANY FALSE INFORMATION ON THIS APPLICATION MAY BE GROUNDS FOR NOT HIRING ME.

Signature

Date *(mm/dd/yy)* _____ / _____ / _____

Lights, Camera, Action!

ROLE PLAY: JOB INTERVIEW

Work in pairs. Choose a job from one of the ads on pages 128-129. Assign someone to be the applicant and the other person to be the interviewer/employer. Create a dialogue and act it out in class. Use the questions and application form on pages 136-137.

Be a Detective

Underline and correct the errors in the sentences below. There could be more than one error in each item.

Ex: I didn't get the job ~~whereas~~ *because* it's too far from my house.

1. Ruby is very smart because her brother always flunks his courses.

2. My colleague won't come to work tomorrow if he feels better.

3. I will go to the party whether or not Randy will go.

4. Because Eddie failed his exam, he repeat the course.

5. Although Lori walked 10 blocks yesterday, she will get to school early.

6. My aunt visit me in the US only if I pay for her ticket.

7. Marissa will quit working unless she doesn't get the promotion she's expecting.

8. You can call my secretary in case you needs help.

9. Even if I will have a lot of money, I will still work.

10. Unless they will pay me more, I will quit my job.

Let's Debate!

Form two groups and debate one of the topics below in class.

- Educational attainment should be a major factor in promotion
- Married women should not work after giving birth. They should focus on their families
- Experience is more important than education

Let's Google it!

Research one of the following

Suggested topics:
- The five current highest-paying jobs
- Most in-demand jobs in different countries
- Latest résumé format

Quiz Yourself!

A. Fill in the blanks with the most appropriate idiom from this unit. You can only use each idiom once. Make sure to use the correct verb tense if the idiom contains a verb.

1. A: I wish I had completed my degree in nursing. Most of my friends who work as nurses already own their homes and are even driving brand new cars.

  B: Wow! That means they are really _____.

2. A: Last Monday, I was in a hurry to go home because I didn't want to put more quarters in the parking meter.

  B: That's like every day for you. Let me guess, you forgot to _____ _____ again. Don't complain if you don't get paid for that day.

3. A: I'm tired of being a messenger. I want to work at a computer and wear a suit and tie just like Mr. Allen.

  B: Hmmm... so you want a _____. You'd better do well in college.

4. A: Why did you reject Ernie's marriage proposal?

   B: I just realized that he's the laziest man in the world. I wish I had known earlier that he was such a _____.

5. A: Michael stopped pursuing his degree in computer science. He realized that he was much happier being a security guard.

   B: Why not? Some _____ can be interesting and pay well too.

6. A: What time should I pick you up?

   B: Uhm, let's see. Today I am _____ work at 6 p.m. Want to have dinner?

7. A: Honey, when will you get a job? We're using up our savings.

   B: Just have a little more patience. When I pass my last interview for this secretarial position, I will surely be the one to _____.

8. A: Why is Hazel always yawning and stretching? There's never a time that she's not sleepy.

   B: You have to understand. She doesn't work during the day. She works the _____.

9. A: You know what, I always get deductions taken from my salary.

   B: I told you. Never forget to _____ as soon as you get to work because that's the only way the company knows that you come on time.

10. A: My husband had a hangover again, so he didn't report to work. That means another 8-hour deduction from his salary. Oh my…

   B: Why? Can't he _____ more hours to make it up?

B. From the given choices, fill in the blanks with the most appropriate answer for each item.

1. I can't understand myself. I still love him _____ he's cheated on me several time.

   a. because   b. even though   c. due to the fact that

2. Alejandra's hair is blond, _____ Paula's is black.

   a. due to the fact that   b. in case   c. whereas

3. You can call Peter _____ you need a plumber for a couple of hours.

   a. even if   b. in case   c. unless

4. Henry will quit his bartending job _____ Microsoft hires him.

   a. unless   b. whereas   c. if

5. My mind will never change, Hakan. I will marry you _____ you have a job. I can take care of both of us.

   a. unless   b. because   c. whether or not

C. Fill in the blanks with the correct words:

1. _____ - a person who is trained to compete in a sport
2. _____ - a person who maintains and audits company accounts
3. _____ - a person who makes eyeglasses
4. _____ - a person who makes and alters garments
5. _____ - a person who plans and designs buildings

Check your answers with the class. Count your points and check your score.

POINTS	PERCENTAGE	POINTS
18-20	90% - 100%	Great job!
15-17	75% - 85%	Very good!
13 - 14	65% - 70%	Good!
12 and below	60% - below	Study harder

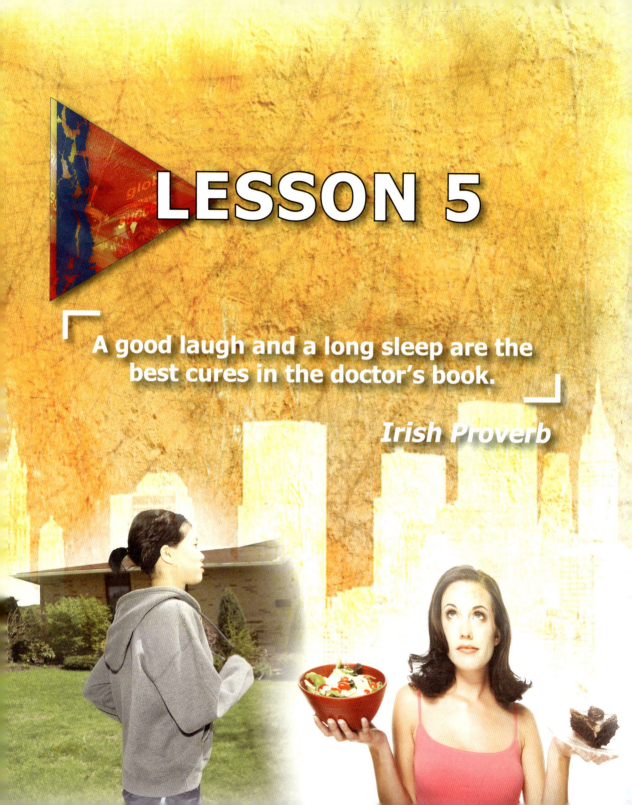

Health

LESSON 5

A. GETTING THE PICTURE : Discuss the following questions in groups of three. Answer in complete sentences.

1. Which food types are considered unhealthy? Why are they considered unhealthy? How does each one of them affect your body? Do you eat or drink any?

2. What do you think is the most effective way to lose weight? Have you ever taken diet pills?

3. Do you exercise? Who should exercise? Why? Which types of exercises are recommended?

4. How often do you get sick? Do you see a doctor regularly?

5. Do you believe in supplements, vitamins and drugs? Do you depend on them when you're in pain or not feeling well?

Jigsaw

B. READING: Work with your group on the assigned paragraph and underline any new vocabulary. Use an English dictionary to look up the meanings. Report your findings to the other groups.

A Healthy Brain is the Key to Living a Happy, Fulfilling and Pain-free Life

Is your memory as good as it used to be? Do you tend to lose your concentration or sometimes search for words to express yourself? Do you feel that your mind is not as sharp as it was before? If you feel that you have these symptoms, you may be a victim of the widespread epidemic of brain fatigue. This condition is officially called age-related memory decline, and lots of people are experiencing this declining cognitive function at an early age.

Our gray matter, also known as our brain, can be our greatest friend or worst foe. If it's working, we have the ability to think clearly, imagine, dream, sense, and do problem solving. On the other hand, if it isn't doing its job, we may feel unhappy, confused, and forgetful; thus, life becomes a struggle. A person's brain is about 3 pounds of mainly fat and water. It is a complex organ, and the least self-regenerative. It is considered to be the most energy-expensive organ since it hardwires neural connections every minute. On a sedentary day, it consumes about 40% of all the calories we eat, thinking an estimated 60,000 thoughts!

So how do we keep our brains healthy? Just like the way we service our cars, keep our muscles firm and bodies trim, we must also take care of our brains. Our brains depend on a constant supply of the right nutrients. Eating essential fats and foods rich in vitamins, minerals and antioxidants, eating enough protein, and avoiding refined carbohydrates, sugar, and excess caffeine and alcohol are ways of keeping our brains healthy and razor sharp. Answer the questions on the next page to find out how healthy your brain is.

C. MIND and MEMORY CHECK:

Answer the questions below by checking ☑ either "Yes" or "No." Each "Yes" answer counts for 1 point. At the end, add up all points and read the scoring.

1. Does it take you a long time to learn things? ☐ YES ☐ NO
2. Do you sometimes lose your train of thought? ☐ YES ☐ NO
3. Do you often misplace things (such as your car keys)? ☐ YES ☐ NO
4. Do you often repeat things to yourself? ☐ YES ☐ NO
5. Do you find it difficult to concentrate? ☐ YES ☐ NO
6. Do you often experience mental exhaustion? ☐ YES ☐ NO
7. Do you often get confused? ☐ YES ☐ NO
8. Do you often forget names? ☐ YES ☐ NO
9. Do you find it hard to add up numbers without writing them down? ☐ YES ☐ NO
10. Do you often forget what you are looking for? ☐ YES ☐ NO
11. Do you often forget what you are about to say? ☐ YES ☐ NO

12. Do you ever forget what day of the week it is?	☐ YES	☐ NO
13. Do you often remember things from the past but forget what you did yesterday?	☐ YES	☐ NO
14. Is your memory deteriorating?	☐ YES	☐ NO

SCORING

Below 5 – you don't have a major problem with your memory.

5 to 10 – your memory needs a boost; you are starting to suffer from brain fatigue

More than 10 – you are experiencing significant memory decline and need to do something about it

D. READING COMPREHENSION: Discuss the following questions in your groups. Report your answers to the class.

Group Work

1. What is "brain fatigue?" Give the characteristics of a person with brain fatigue.

    _____

2. How much does a brain weigh? What are its functions?

    _____

3. How many calories does a brain consume on a sedentary day?

    _____

4. Why is our gray matter considered to be the most energy-expensive organ in our body?

_____

5. How can we keep our brains healthy?

_____

E. VOCABULARY PRACTICE: Match the words with their definitions by using contextual clues (Figuring out the meaning of the word by the way it was used in a sentence.) Compare your answers with your partner. Identify whether the words are adjectives, nouns, verbs or adverbs.

COLUMN A	COLUMN B
1. symptom __f__ __noun__	a. widespread occurence of a disease/condition
2. epidemic ___ ___	b. enemy
3. decline ___ ___	c. inactive
4. cognitive ___ ___	d. fail, weaken, drop
5. foe ___ ___	e. connected or incorporated by or as if by permanent electrical connections
6. complex ___ ___	f. indication/sign
7. regenerate ___ ___	g. involving conscious intellectual activity
8. sedentary ___ ___	h. complicated, difficult
9. hardwired ___ ___	i. to form or create again
10. antioxidants ___ ___	j. substances (such as beta-carotene or vitamin C) that inhibit oxidation or reactions promoted by oxygen, peroxides, or free radicals

F. HOMEWORK: Search for an article related to a health issue (for example: the newest kinds of cancer treatment). Read it and share your findings and opinions in class.

IDIOMS

A. Work with your partner. Read the letters below and figure out the meaning of all idioms by discussing them with your partner. Pick out two idioms and explain them in front of the class.

Dear Dr. Phil,

I'll be attending my high school reunion in 3 months. I haven't seen my former classmates in ages! My wife, who was my high school sweetheart, is very excited to go, but I'm not. I have gained a lot of weight over the years, and I've been trying to *be in shape*, but nothing has happened. I've *been on several diets*, but the pounds I lost just kept coming back. I actually feel insecure because I'm married to a gorgeous woman, and I don't want to be ridiculed at our high school reunion. My goal for the next 3 months is not to *put on weight*. Please help me! I really want to look my best and make my wife proud of me.

From: Chubby Hubby

Dear Dr. Phil,

I keep *coming down with* a cold. I have tried all sorts of cold remedies and I take vitamins but still nothing works. I *feel run-down* from lack of sleep. Because of this, I have been absent from work a lot. At my last checkup, the doctor said that there was nothing we could do but let the cold virus *run its course*. I am starting to feel hopeless. How can I *get over* this cold?!

From: Sneezing in Miami

ZONI LANGUAGE CENTERS ©

Dear Dr. Phil,

I am a member of the swim team at my school. I have practice every other day. Lately, I have noticed that after a few laps, I need to **catch my breath**. This never happened to me before. I always **warm up** before jumping into the pool and **cool off** after my routine. I gained a couple of pounds last month, but I was able to **work them off**. My coach has been a big help to me in losing the weight I gained. I plan to compete in the next tournament, but I won't be able to win if I easily get tired after a few laps in the water. I really need your help.

Swimming Enthusiast

Dear Dr. Phil,

I'm 25 years old and I work as a bartender. I am so conscious of my body that I work out every single day. I **work out** not only to keep in shape but also to **build up** my strength. However, I have been feeling really tired lately. When I go to work, I sometimes feel sleepy and out of sync. The other night my boss got mad at me because I dropped 2 bottles of liquor while mixing my customers' drinks. I don't know if going to the gym is taking its toll on my job. I love bartending but going to the gym is like an addiction for me. I need your advice.

From: Pooped Out

B. DISCOVER THE MEANING: Work with a partner. Match the idioms with their meanings below. You may refer to the letters to help you figure out the answers.

COLUMN A	COLUMN B
1. be in shape _____	a. to gain weight
2. be on a diet _____	b. to control food consumption in order to lose weight
3. put on weight _____	c. to develop an illness
4. work out _____	d. to increase muscle size and strength gradually
5. warm up _____	e. to loosen the muscles before exercising
6. build up _____	f. to stop exercising in order to breathe more normally
7. catch one's breath _____	g. to do physical exercise, such as lifting weights
8. work off _____	h. to continue for an expected period of time
9. cool off _____	i. to remove or to get rid of
10. feel run-down _____	j. to be in good physical condition
11. come down with _____	k. to be tired and in poor physical condition
12. run its course _____	l. to cool down after strenuous exercise
13. get over _____	m. to recover from an illness

Party Time

Walk around the classroom and interview your classmates. Answer in complete sentences using the idioms and correct verb tenses. Write down the answers in the blanks.

Example: Have you had the measles? If yes, how did you pass the time until the disease *ran its course*?

____Avi____: I stayed home alone until the measles ran its course.

1. Are you in shape? If yes, what do you do to **be in shape**?

   _____:_____.

2. Have you ever **been on a diet**? Was it successful?

   _____:_____.

3. What causes people to **put on weight**?

   _____:_____.

4. Why is it important to **warm up** before doing exercises and **cool down** afterwards?

   _____:_____.

PAGE 152   ZONI LANGUAGE CENTERS ©

5. What do most people do to **build up** their strength?

_____ : _____ .

6. Do you exercise? If yes, how often do you **work out**?

_____ : _____ .

7. If you feel **run-down**, what do you normally do?

_____ : _____ .

8. What do you think is an excellent way of **working off** your tension or stress from work?

_____ : _____ .

9. What is the easiest way to **get over** fatigue?

_____ : _____ .

10. What is the first thing you do when you feel that you're **coming down with** the flu?

_____ : _____ .

WRITING: Pretend that you are Dr. Phil. Choose one of the letters on pages 149-150 and write an advice letter. Use as many idioms as possible. Read your letter to the class.

Game: "GUESSTURES"

Listen to your teacher's instructions.

Homework

Fill in the blanks with the appropriate idioms and use the correct tenses. Compare your answers with a partner.

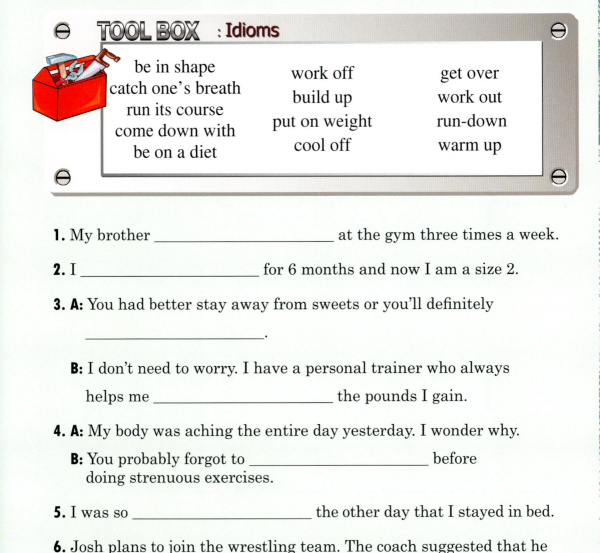

TOOL BOX : Idioms

be in shape
catch one's breath
run its course
come down with
be on a diet

work off
build up
put on weight
cool off

get over
work out
run-down
warm up

1. My brother _____ at the gym three times a week.

2. I _____ for 6 months and now I am a size 2.

3. **A:** You had better stay away from sweets or you'll definitely _____.

   B: I don't need to worry. I have a personal trainer who always helps me _____ the pounds I gain.

4. **A:** My body was aching the entire day yesterday. I wonder why.

   B: You probably forgot to _____ before doing strenuous exercises.

5. I was so _____ the other day that I stayed in bed.

6. Josh plans to join the wrestling team. The coach suggested that he should _____ his strength by lifting weights.

7. **A:** Hurry up! We are way behind in the marathon.

   B: Hold on! I need to _____. We've been running for 8 miles already.

8. Breathing exercises are a good way to _____ after a strenuous work out.

9. **Patient:** Doc, what should I do to _____ this cold?

   Doctor: Well, there isn't a cure for the common cold. You just have to let the cold virus _____. I can give you medicine to relieve your congestion.

Lights, Camera, Action!

See Teacher's Manual

ROLE PLAY: Work in pairs and create your own dialogue using the idioms on page 155. Pretend one of you is a doctor and the other one is the patient.

Practice! Then... perform!

NOUN CLAUSES WITH VERBS & ADJECTIVES
Let's Break The Ice

LESSON 5

A. On a small piece of paper, write your name, fold it and give it to your teacher. Then your teacher will have you pick a name from the collected papers.

B. Now, complete the sentences in the box below about the classmate you picked. Don't tell anyone who you got.

SECRET NAME: _____

1. I *think* that he/she _____

2. I *know* that he/she _____

3. I *found out* that he/she _____

4. I am *amazed* that he/she _____

5. I am *sure* that he/she _____

C. Now read your sentences to class and have the class guess who it is!

Noun Clauses with Adjectives and Verbs

Noun clauses can be used with adjectives and verbs. See the examples below:

Noun Clauses with Adjectives

Adjective + **(that)** + Clause

Examples

Clara was **surprised** that *size 2 fits me*. She thinks *I'm fat*!

I am **aware** that *I have put on too much weight*.

My parents are **happy** that *you are my fiancée*.

Other adjectives you can use with noun clauses:

sure	clear	worried	angry	afraid
disappointed	sorry	aware	glad	scary
amazed	certain	obvious	surprised	

Noun Clauses with Verbs

Verbs + **(that)** + Clause

Examples

Robert **knows** that *he needs to see the doctor soon*.

People **must understand** that *drugs should not be abused*.

Doctors **believe** that *vitamins are essential*.

Other verbs you can use with noun clauses:

believe	regret	hope	find out	realize
forget	dream	notice	expect	understand
learn	decide	show	know	think

Group Work

Share your opinion by responding to each sentence with:

> "I **think** that ..." / "I **don't think** that ..."
> "I **believe** that ..." / "I **don't believe** that ..."

Example: Vitamins are essential.

Student A: I think (that) we also should watch our diet.
Student B: I believe that exercise is more important.
Student C: I don't think that exercise works if we don't eat properly.

1. People don't have to go to the gym to get fit.

2. Paying for a personal trainer is a waste of money.

3. Coffee is harmful.

4. It is important to keep fit to have a healthy marriage.

5. We should read the nutrition information on food packaging.

6. Bread is better than rice.

7. The government should eliminate sales of fast food to encourage people to eat healthier food.

8. It's healthy to have a glass of wine every day.

9. Vegetables should be a part of a healthy diet.

10. It's better to drink juice than soda.

Pair Practice

Write the verb or adjective that will best complete each sentence below. If it's a verb, use the appropriate tense.

1. We _____ that we should watch our diet.

2. Don't _____ that it's my birthday tomorrow.

3. Sheila _____ that if she fails the exam, she has to repeat the course.

4. Danny was _____ that in spite of daily exercise, he didn't lose weight this week.

5. Yuki is _____ that her boyfriend is serious about her.

6. Don't you _____ that your eating fast food every day is the reason for your weight gain?

7. It's _____ that she's got a crush on you. She's always smiling at you and never fails to greet you every day.

8. We _____ that knowledge is power!

9. Yesterday, I _____ that Ronnie was sent to the emergency room.

10. The teacher was _____ that many students failed the course.

Party Time

Stand up and complete the sentences below with your classmates' names and noun clauses.

1. _____ believes that it is necessary to measure the food that we eat.

2. _____ doesn't think exercise works for him/her.

3. _____ noticed that he/she's been losing weight recently.

4. _____ is worried about his/her current weight.

5. _____ realized that he/she is not eating a healthy diet.

6. _____ is not aware that it's necessary to have a flu shot every year.

7. _____ is disappointed with his/her own eating habits.

8. _____ doesn't believe that diet pills are harmful.

9. _____ hopes to gain more muscle mass.

10. _____ is glad that he/she is in perfect shape.

Homework

Complete the sentences.

1. My father agrees that _____.

2. Our teacher is sometimes disappointed that _____.

3. Recently, I've realized that _____.

4. When I was young, my mother was astonished that _____.

5. We should all be glad that _____.

LESSON 5: Kill it or Keep

COMMUNICATING EFFECTIVELY: Work with a partner and come up with two dialogues. One is to show how to keep the conversation going while the other shows how to kill it.

TOPIC: I dropped 80 lbs. I feel so healthy!

KILLER RESPONSE: Oh ok. Whatever!

KEEPER RESPONSE: Oh wow! Share your secret!

Jigsaw

Below is a chart for you to fill out. Work with two group mates, then report your completed chart to the class.

REASONS TO KILL CONVERSATION

Example: Topic is boring.

1. _____
2. _____
3. _____
4. _____
5. _____

REASONS TO KEEP CONVERSATION

Example: You like the person you're talking to.

1. _____
2. _____
3. _____
4. _____
5. _____

EXPRESSIONS TO KILL THE CONVERSATION

Example: Uhm. I don't know.

1. _____
2. _____
3. _____
4. _____
5. _____

EXPRESSIONS TO KEEP CONVERSATION

Example: How do you feel about it?

1. _____
2. _____
3. _____
4. _____
5. _____

Stand Up

Using noun clauses with adjectives/verbs, come up with a statement about health or nutrition. Then share it with two classmates who should respond by keeping and killing the conversation. Work with as many different classmates as you can. Note: Refer to the table below for more suggested keepers and killers.

Student A: I believe that it's harder to lose weight when you're older.

Student B: I think so, too. In fact, I'm kind of experiencing that right now. **(KEEPER)**
Student C: I have no idea about that. **(KILLER)**

YOUR TOPIC: _____

CONVERSATION KILLERS	CONVERSATION KEEPERS
I have no idea. Whatever!	Tell me more about that.
No comment.	What do you think?
I don't know.	I agree/disagree. In fact,…
I'd rather not comment about that.	How do you feel about it?
I'm not really interested.	That's interesting!
I'd rather talk about (give another topic).	I think so too.
	Wow! Tell me more about it.

LESSON 5

What's wrong?

Work individually and figure out if each sentence is CORRECT or INCORRECT. Check the appropriate box for each sentence.

1. I don't know what is your name.

☐ CORRECT ☐ INCORRECT

2. Do you know where the nearest gym is?

☐ CORRECT ☐ INCORRECT

3. I can't tell you who do I like.

☐ CORRECT ☐ INCORRECT

4. Jenny can't remember when she started at Zoni.

☐ CORRECT ☐ INCORRECT

5. Please tell me why do you love me.

☐ CORRECT ☐ INCORRECT

6. I can't understand how you survived without eating dinner last night.

☐ CORRECT ☐ INCORRECT

7. I have no idea how much does a new BMW costs.

☐ CORRECT ☐ INCORRECT

8. I wonder do you exercise every day.

☐ CORRECT ☐ INCORRECT

9. I don't remember if I locked the door before I left.

☐ CORRECT ☐ INCORRECT

10. I'm not sure whether the managers like the program.

☐ CORRECT ☐ INCORRECT

Now listen to your teacher for the correct answers. For every correct answer, give yourself 1 point.

RESULTS

0-2 points – You may face some challenges in forming and using noun clauses, but the good news is that now you have an excellent chance to learn this structure, so you have to pay extra attention to your teacher and participate well in group and pair practices.

3-4 points – You have some idea on how to correctly use noun clauses but it is challenging for you to maintain the correct form. It is therefore important that you pay more attention to the structure and practice its use.

5-6 points – Sometimes you use noun clauses correctly and sometimes you don't. You need to review the structure and make sure to practice its use in both written and oral forms.

7-8 points – You know how to form and use noun clauses and will find the lesson quite easy but fun! You need just a little review of the structure and make sure that every sentence you produce is correct, especially in conversation.

9-10 points – You are considered an expert in noun clauses and you can help your teacher teach your classmates!

Noun Clauses with Embedded Questions I

Below is a guide on the use and form of noun clauses with questions. Study the table to figure out how noun clauses are used with questions.

Noun Clause with Information Questions

Noun clause + Information Question { what, who/whom, when, why, where, which, how }

Examples

Information Questions	Noun Clause with Information Questions
Where is our teacher?	I don't know **where** *our teacher is*.
Where does Hakan buy vitamins?	I don't remember **where** *he buys vitamins*.
When is Lyka's birthday?	Please tell me **when** *Lyka's birthday is*.
When does Janice go to the gym?	Can you tell me **when** *Janice goes to the gym*?
What is your phone number?	I can't tell you **what** *my phone number is*.
What did you do yesterday?	I won't tell you **what** *I did yesterday*.
How do you stay in shape?	It's hard to say **how** *I stay in shape*.
Whom do you love?	I can't tell you **whom** *I love*.

Noun Clauses with Embedded Questions II

Noun Clause with Information Questions + Modals

Noun Clause + Information Question + Modal

Examples

Information Question with Modals	Noun Clause + Information question with Modals
Where will you work out?	You need to decide **where** you **will** work out.
When can you cook for me?	I am not sure **when** I **can** cook for you.
What time should I give you a ring?	Can you tell me **what** time I **should** give you a ring?

Noun Clauses with Embedded Questions III

Noun clause with Yes/No Questions

Noun clause + if / whether + Yes/No Questions

Examples

Yes/No Questions	Noun clause with Yes/No Questions
Does your brother smoke?	I don't know **if** my brother smokes.
Did Mario use to work as a personal trainer?	I have no idea **whether** Mario used to work as a personal trainer.
Can I give you a buzz this weekend?	I can't tell you yet **if** you can call me this weekend.
Will Mr. Brooks register for aerobics classes next month?	I'm not sure **whether** Mr. Brooks will register for aerobics classes next month.

Chain Drill

See Teacher's Manual

Everybody stands up and forms a circle. Student A starts with the first question and student B answers. Then, student B asks the next question and student C answers. Continue until everybody in the group has asked and answered using noun clauses. Have fun!

Student A: Where can I lease exercise equipment?

Student B: I don't know _____.

Student B: Are you satisfied with your job?

Student C: I'm not sure _____.

Student C: What time is the next aerobics class?

Student D: I don't know _____.

Student D: Do you like your figure?

Student E: I'm not sure _____.

Student E: Did you lose weight?

Student F: I also wonder _____.

Student F: When did you start kickboxing?

Student G: I can't remember _____.

Student G: Where will you eat dinner?

Student H: I haven't decided _____.

Student H: What time did the training start?

Student I: Let me ask Donna _____.

Student I: Where has Robert been?

Student J: I can't tell you _____.

Student J: Have you tried Korean green tea?

Student K: I don't remember _____.

Student K: What time will Jeremy meet us to go jogging?

Student L: Yeah, we need to know _____.

Student L: Should I invest in a spa business?

Student M: I have no idea _____.

Student M: How can I lose weight within a week?

Student N: Well, I'd also like to know _____.

Student N: Have you ever considered taking diet pills?

Student O: I don't remember _____.

Student O: Is Jessica enjoying her new career as a gym instructor?

Student P: I wonder _____.

Pair Practice
Student A

A. Interview your partner with questions below.

1. Where does your teacher work out?
2. What's your best friend's name?
3. When will you retire?
4. Where did you buy those vitamins?
5. How much is the monthly gym membership?

B. Give complete answers to your partner using **Noun Clauses** provided below.

1. I don't know…
2. I'm not sure…
3. I also wonder…
4. We need to know…
5. I can't remember…

Pair Practice

Student B

A. Give complete answers to your partner using the **Noun Clauses** provided below.

1. I don't know…

2. I don't remember…

3. I'm not sure…

4. I can't tell you…

5. Please tell me…

B. Interview your partner with questions below.

1. How is your boyfriend doing?

2. Where will you spend your next vacation?

3. What time does your mother eat breakfast?

4. How many minutes should we exercise every day?

5. Where did your brother learn English?

Round Robin Story

Work in groups of four and make up a story using as many noun clauses as possible. Each member of the group must contribute ideas. Assign a member of the group to write down the sentences.

Example:

Student A: Chuckie wonders how green tea works in our body.

Student B: He doesn't know where it comes from.

Student C: He wants to know if it really helps in losing weight.

Student D: He can't understand how a simple bag of leaves dipped in hot water cleanses toxins from our body.

Student A: He believes all these ads about the booming green tea business are mistaken.

Student B: So one day,...

Homework

Research interesting health products available on the market. Select one interesting health product available on the market and do a presentation in class. In your presentation, include what the product can cure or why it is considered good for you. Use samples of the product or visual aids to support your presentation.

LEND ME YOUR EARS

 Listen to your teacher read the sentences. If it contains a noun clauses, circle YES. If the sentence does not contain a noun clause, circle NO.

1.	☐ YES	☐ NO	6.	☐ YES	☐ NO
2.	☐ YES	☐ NO	7.	☐ YES	☐ NO
3.	☐ YES	☐ NO	8.	☐ YES	☐ NO
4.	☐ YES	☐ NO	9.	☐ YES	☐ NO
5.	☐ YES	☐ NO	10.	☐ YES	☐ NO

Conversation Practice

Write a sentence about HEALTH that you strongly believe in, using a noun clause (with adjective or verb or with embedded questions). Report your statement to two group mates who in turn will keep and kill the conversation. Rotate roles until everybody in the group has reported his/her statement.

Student A: I strongly believe that it's essential to take vitamins every day.

Student B: Oh I think so too! In fact I take them every day. (**KEEPER**)
Student C: Oh well, I have no opinion. (**KILLER**)

YOUR TOPIC: _____

Present in class!

Drawing

A. Draw an image of your favorite person or object.

B. WRITING: Write an explanation of the image you drew on page 175. Use noun clauses and idioms in your composition. Be ready to share your writing in front of the class.

Be a Detective

Find the mistakes and correct them in the sentences below. Compare your corrections with your partner.

Example: I'm not sure when ~~did he arrive~~ *he arrived* in Canada.

1. My dad notice that I have been gaining weight.

2. Barry wants to know when is my birthday.

3. Can you tell me where do you live?

4. I don't know why did he leave his country.

5. We are aware that English important is.

6. I want to know whether the gym do they accepts credit card.

7. Please tell me what is his phone number! Please!

8. My cousin isn't sure what bus number should he take.

9. Let me know if will you come to the party?

10. I wonder how did my neighbor lose a great deal of weight within a month.

Let's Debate!

Form two groups and debate one of the topics below in class.

- Liposuction should be banned
- Diet pills must be forbidden everywhere in the world
- Smoking should be made illegal
- The legal age for drinking alcohol should be lowered

Let's Google it!

Research one of the following

Suggested topics:

- Research the latest trends in losing weight. What are the side effects? How much would it cost? Are the testimonials real? Present your findings in class.

- Find out the latest research on a health issue. Are there diseases that are more common nowadays? Where do they come from? What are the doctors' points of view? Who should be cautious about these diseases?

Share your research in class!

Quiz Yourself!

A. IDIOMS: Circle the letter of the word or phrase that is synonymous to the idiom.

1. be in shape
    a. wear a body girdle
    b. have a round body
    c. be in good physical condition

2. catch one's breath
    a. stop exercising to breathe normally
    b. catch air
    c. exhale

3. work out
    a. work out of the house
    b. do physical exercise
    c. work extremely long hours

4. build up
    a. to increase strength and muscle size
    b. to construct something
    c. to create

5. cool off
    a. break up temporarily
    b. be as cool as a cucumber
    c. to lose heat or warmth from the body

B. Provide the correct answer for each question.

1. How long will it take me to master this grammar point?

    I don't know _____

2. When is spring break?

    I don't know _____

3. How much will it cost to register for classes this summer?

I don't know _____

4. Will he be our gym instructor next semester?

I'm not sure _____

5. Did she get a tummy tuck instead of going on a diet?

I have no idea _____

C. Complete the sentences using the clauses given.

1. Drinking coffee is good for one's health.

I don't believe _____

2. Undergoing liposuction is the best way to get rid of fat.

I doubt that _____

3. All the students know where the library is.

The teacher assumed _____

4. Everyone will pass the course with flying colors.

We hope _____

5. They will certainly win the trophy in the finals.

I am sure _____

D. VOCABULARY: Complete the sentences using the correct word from the box.

| symptom/s | sedentary | foe | epidemic | complex |

1. One of the _____ of the flu is body aches.

2. Is it possible for your best friend to be your greatest _____?

3. This grammar lesson isn't as _____ as I thought it would be.

4. There was an _____ in China so flights going to that country were cancelled.

5. It is not advisable to be _____. You will definitely gain weight if you don't do some form of exercise.

Check your answers with the class. Count your points and check your score.

POINTS	PERCENTAGE	POINTS
18-20	90% - 100%	Great job!
15-17	75% - 85%	Very good!
13 - 14	65% - 70%	Good!
12 and below	60% - below	Study harder

Oral Exam

Choose from one of the topics below. Then prepare a 2-minute dialogue in groups of three using the following:

1. Grammar points learned from the book
2. Conversation strategies from each unit
3. At least 10 idioms from the book

Practice your conversation. Then present to the class. Thank you.

TOPICS:

1. Immigration
2. Health
3. Education
4. Career
5. Technology

Congratulations!

You have moved on to the next level — High Intermediate Course, Express Yourself.

APPENDIX
▶ VERB LIST

REGULAR VERBS

Verb	Simple Past	Past Participle
LESSON 1		
evolve	evolved	evolved
install	installed	installed
approve	approved	approved
pursue	pursued	pursued
organize	organized	organized
suggest	suggested	suggested
attend	attended	attended
propose	proposed	proposed
replace	replaced	replaced
LESSON 2		
expect	expected	expected
earn	earned	earned
adjust	adjusted	adjusted
afford	afforded	afforded
apply	applied	applied
discuss	discussed	discussed
encounter	encountered	encountered
decide	decided	decided
gain	gained	gained
stay	stayed	stayed
notice	noticed	noticed
purchase	purchased	purchased
graduate	graduated	graduated
retire	retired	retired
inherit	inherited	inherited
return	returned	returned
volunteer	volunteered	volunteered
complete	completed	completed
change	changed	changed
LESSON 3		
involve	involved	involved
require	required	required
join	joined	joined
enroll	enrolled	enrolled
intend	intended	intended
pass	passed	passed
prepare	prepared	prepared
offer	offered	offered
finish	finished	finished

Verb	Simple Past	Past Participle
expand	expanded	expanded
repeat	repeated	repeated
land	landed	landed
explain	explained	explained
admit	admitted	admitted
solve	solved	solved
arrive	arrived	arrived
receive	received	received
LESSON 4		
maintain	maintained	maintained
audit	audited	audited
train	trained	trained
hire	hired	hired
alter	altered	altered
compose	composed	composed
terminate	terminated	terminated
rehearse	rehearsed	rehearsed
contribute	contributed	contributed
inform	informed	informed
establish	established	established
respond	responded	responded
inquire	inquired	inquired
conduct	conducted	conducted
promote	promoted	promoted
fulfill	fulfilled	fulfilled
fail	failed	failed
complain	complained	complained
LESSON 5		
exercise	exercised	exercised
believe	believe	believe
depend	depend	depend
consume	consumed	consumed
compete	competed	competed
suggest	suggested	suggested
relieve	relieved	relieved
realize	realized	realized
remember	remembered	remembered
survive	survived	survived
register	registered	registered
invest	invested	invested
assume	assumed	assumed

APPENDIX
▶ VERB LIST

IRREGULAR VERBS

Verb	Simple Past	Past Participle	Verb	Simple Past	Past Participle
LESSON 1			**LESSON 3**		
buy	bought	bought	tell	told	told
quit	quit	quit	forget	forgot	forgotten
leave	left	left	read	read	read
get	got	gotten	know	knew	known
find	found	found	hold	held	held
lay	laid	laid	begin	began	begun
speak	spoke	spoken	mean	meant	meant
pay	paid	paid	put	put	put
meet	met	met	hit	hit	hit
see	saw	seen	sleep	slept	slept
withdraw	withdrew	withdrawn	throw	threw	thrown
broadcast	broadcast	broadcast	buy	bought	bought
LESSON 2			hang	hung	hung
choose	chose	chosen	**LESSON 4**		
understand	understood	understood	fit	fit	fit
break	broke	broken	write	wrote	written
become	became	become	win	won	won
think	thought	thought	stand	stood	stood
say	said	said	bring	brought	brought
shake	shook	shaken	buy	bought	bought
do	did	done	spend	spent	spent
hear	heard	heard	go	went	gone
give	gave	given	send	sent	sent
lose	lost	lost	seek	sought	sought
set	set	set	grow	grew	grown
take	took	taken	make	made	made
catch	caught	caught	get	got	gotten
fall	fell	fallen	wear	wore	worn
feel	felt	felt	**LESSON 5**		
show	showed	shown	eat	ate	eaten
fly	flew	flown	drink	drank	drunk
steal	stole	stolen	build	built	built
blow	blew	blown	give	gave	given
sell	sold	sold	cost	cost	cost
			undergo	underwent	undergone

PHRASAL VERBS AND IDIOMS

Phrasal Verb & Idiom	Meaning
LESSON 1	
be meaning to	to have always planned to do
run into	to meet by chance
collect dust	to remain unused for a long time
pack rat	someone who keeps items that are not useful anymore
tough cookie	someone who is stubborn, or hard to get along with
get along	to have a good relationship with
pay off	to completely pay a debt
pay someone back	to return what someone owes
put up with	to be patient with
be fed up with	to be tired of something
LESSON 2	
I don't get it	I don't understand.
follow someone	to understand someone
hope for the best	to hope for good things to happen
shake one's head	to show disagreement or confusion
for the sake of	for the benefit of something or someone
pros and cons	advantages and disadvantages
in demand	in need/greatly needed
make a living	to earn enough money to live well
greener pastures	a better or more promising situation
LESSON 3	
pass with flying colors	pass something easily and with a high score
Ivy League school	a small group of older and famous eastern United States colleges and universities such as Harvard, Yale and Princeton
as easy as ABC	very easy
bookworm	someone who reads a lot
work your way through college	work at a job to help pay for your college or university expenses
hit the books	to begin to study hard
put on your thinking cap	start thinking in a serious manner
smart cookie	a clever or intelligent person

PHRASAL VERBS AND IDIOMS

Phrasal Verb & Idiom	Meaning
teacher's pet	the teacher's favorite student
honor roll	a list of people/students who have done exceptionally well
learn in a snap	to learn very fast

Lesson 4

Phrasal Verb & Idiom	Meaning
do for a living	have as a job
make a living	to have a job; to earn money
white-collar job	a job having to do with an office environment
blue-collar job	a job having to do with a non-office work environment
put in	to spend time at work
clock in	indicate specific time to start work
clock out	indicate specific time to finish work
get off (work)	to leave work at the end of the workday
couch potato	a lazy inactive person who spends a great deal of time watching television
bring home the bacon	to earn a living, especially for a family
graveyard shift	an eight-hour work period through the early morning hours

Lesson 5

Phrasal Verb & Idiom	Meaning
be in shape	to be in good physical condition
put on weight	to gain weight
come down with	to develop an illness
feel run-down	to be tired and in poor physical condition
run its course	to continue for an expected period of time
catch one's breath	to stop exercising in order to breathe more normally
warm up	to loosen body muscles before exercising
cool off	to cool down after strenuous exercise
work off	to get rid of extra weight by exercise
build up	to increase muscle size and strength
work out	to do physical exercise
be on a diet	to control food consumption in order to lose weight
get over	to recover from an illness